THE SMITHSONIAN INSTITUTION

A WORLD OF DISCOVERY

THE SMITHSONIAN INSTITUTION

A WORLD OF DISCOVERY

An Exploration of Behind-the-Scenes Research in the Arts, Sciences and Humanities

THE SMITHSONIAN INSTITUTION: A WORLD OF DISCOVERY

Author: Mark Bello
Contributors: William Schulz, Madeleine Jacobs, James Cornell, Susan Bliss, Thomas Harney, William Moss
Editors: William Schulz, Madeleine Jacobs, Alvin Rosenfeld
Project Coordinator: Kathryn Lindeman
Photo Editor: Lilas Wiltshire
Editorial Assistants: Jacqueline Lovett, Natalie Fielman, Holly Hammett
Production Consultants: Alan Burchell, Alan Carter, Paula Dailey
Designers: Meadows & Wiser
Distributed by Smithsonian Institution Press

This publication was made possible through the generosity of the James Smithson Society; the Smithsonian's Assistant Secretaries
for the Sciences, the Arts and Humanities, Education and Public Service, and External Affairs; and Smithsonian Institution trust funds.
The Office of Public Affairs thanks Robert S. Hoffmann for his support throughout the project.

The Smithsonian Institution was founded nearly 150 years ago with the remarkable gift of a private individual, establishing a tradition that has persisted over time through thousands of financial contributions from the private sector—individuals, corporations and foundations—as well as foreign nations, to make possible imaginative programs not otherwise funded by annual federal appropriations. In accepting James Smithson's unprecedented legacy to the United States of America, the government undertook trusteeship of this Institution, an obligation for all time to maintain and foster basic institutional needs.

More recently, especially in the past decade, vital and innovative programs and activities have been created, largely without federal subsidy. Such admirable extensions of the Institution have well served James Smithson's testamentary wish for the "increase and diffusion of knowledge among men."

To this end, the Smithsonian will continue its efforts to supplement federal support for basic necessities, encouraging the dedicated participation of the private sector in the work of the Institution so as to make possible still greater progress in creative, imaginative contributions toward the increase and diffusion of knowledge.

Individuals will find a variety of opportunities to become part of this world of discovery through individual philanthropic efforts organized by the Smithsonian Institution's Office of Development. For more information, write to Office of Development, Smithsonian Institution, Washington, D.C. 20560.

Library of Congress Cataloging-in-Publication Data
Office of Public Affairs.
   The Smithsonian Institution, a world of discovery: an exploration
of behind-the-scenes research in the arts, sciences, and humanities /
[author, Mark Bello; contributors, William Schulz . . . et al.; editors,
William Schulz, Madeleine Jacobs, Alvin Rosenfeld].
       p.   cm.
   ISBN 1-56098-314-0 (acid-free paper)
   1. Smithsonian Institution. 2. Science museums — Washington
(D.C.) I. Schulz, William. II. Smithsonian Institution. III. Title.
Q11.B45 1993   93-14987
069'.09753—dc20   CIP

Front cover: One of the many research projects at the Smithsonian Astrophyiscal Observatory yielded this digital image of the M27 Nebula, known as the Dumbbell Nebula. (Photo by Rudolph Schild)
Half-title page: These steel and brass "Portal Gates," commissioned for the Renwick Gallery in 1972 and hand-forged by artist Albert Paley, are installed at the entrance to the gallery's museum shop.
Frontispiece: Smithsonian Tropical Research Institute staff assistant Elizabeth Padrón works underwater to remove damselfish from coral. Follow-up studies determine the re-invasion and coral recovery rates after these and other predators are removed. (Photo by Carl Hansen)
Back cover: Kyoichi Ito, an Oriental art restoration specialist at the Freer and Sackler galleries, replaces a section of a Japanese ceremonial palanquin following conservation. (Photo by John Tsantes)

Contents

FULL OF
WONDER:
THE
SMITHSONIAN
QUEST

An Introduction to the Smithsonian's
World of Discovery

In a crowded room of the original Smithsonian Institution Building,
19th-century scientists inspect and classify specimens.

"The most beautiful experience we have is the mysterious. It is the fundamental emotion that stands at the cradle of true art and true understanding."
—*Albert Einstein*

"Knowledge begins in wonder."—*Inscription that greeted visitors to the Smithsonian's Children's Room, completed in 1901*

A young visitor listens to the "sounds" of a seashell in the Discovery Room, a touchable exhibit for children in the Museum of Natural History. (Photo by Chip Clark)

When we trace trails of human endeavors in art, history and science, seemingly divergent paths eventually converge toward common destinations, vistas where resolution opens new paths and views are still unfolding and ever changing. Each journey concludes and begins anew with deeper understanding and appreciation of the greatest mysteries of all—those of our own existence, the workings of human creativity and the place of humankind in nature. This is the Smithsonian at its most exciting, and this experience is found in research that discovers new paths and opens them to others.

The millions of people who visit the Smithsonian Institution's 15 museums and galleries and the National Zoological Park each year traverse this same terrain. During their journeys, they can enjoy the fruits of human creativity spanning the centuries. They can also review the past, often finding a historical context for assessing the sometimes confusing events of today. These wanderings expose them to unfamiliar social landscapes—the traditions and the material and visual legacies of different cultures—and to nature's diversity, as revealed over evolutionary time or as sampled from different parts of the world.

Exhibitions, however, are simply the public face of the Smithsonian. Behind the scenes, more than 800 specialists and scholars in the arts, humanities and the sciences probe the limits of understanding in their respective fields. Their efforts span the globe, reach into the heavens, plumb the depths of the oceans and extend from the "big bang" some 10 billion to 20 billion years ago into the future.

The connection between any two research activities—say, studies of water quality in the Chesapeake Bay and the analysis of American art at the end of the 19th century—may not be immediately apparent. Yet both follow the Smithsonian's charge, the mandate of James Smithson, the Institution's first benefactor, to search for understanding and to share that understanding with all.

"The Increase and Diffusion of Knowledge"

In his will, the wealthy English scientist specified that his bequest be used to create an institution in Washington for "the increase and diffusion of knowledge." Today's museum visitors are among the beneficiaries of this two-part charge to carry out research and to educate.

"No museum can grow and be respected," George Brown Goode, assistant secretary in charge of the Smithsonian's National Museum, wrote in 1889, "which does not each year give additional proofs of its claims to be considered a center of learning." The scores of new exhibitions mounted each year are evidence of the Institution's scholarly endeavors, although visitors may not recognize the link between research and exhibition. Other proofs are less apparent to even the most dedicated museumgoers. In any given year, Smithsonian researchers publish more than 1,000 books and articles, participate in dozens of research expeditions and collect thousands of specimens and artifacts—from insects and dinosaur bones to aircraft and Asian art. Smithsonian scholars also serve as advisers to national and international agencies, teach courses at universities around the world, and forge cooperative ties with many of the outside experts who come to the Smithsonian each year to study its huge and varied collections or to attend its numerous scholarly conferences and workshops.

The Institution is an active participant, catalyst and leader in efforts to understand the universe, the Earth and human culture. A visit to the office of any researcher is a glimpse of one of the many fascinating subplots woven into this story. A few such visits soon give an appreciation of how many chapters of this story remain to be written and of the vastness of the Smithsonian's research mission. And with each visit, excitement and enthusiasm for the quest grow greater.

We can also begin to see connections that unite the components of the Institution's research program. The desire to discover the unknown and unravel the mysterious explains why, for example, Smithsonian astronomers and engineers develop sophisticated satellite-borne telescopes to peer into the far reaches of the Milky Way and beyond to other galaxies; why Smithsonian botanists endure tropical rains and insects to document life histories of rare New World orchids; why the Institution's art historians and folklorists search across America to identify and preserve rapidly vanishing crafts, arts and oral traditions; and why its scholars and archivists have taken on the chal-

lenges of inventorying all of the hundreds of thousands of American paintings completed before 1914 and all sculptures and all portraits in the United States.

A Smithsonian Sampler

In these pages, you will read about a sample of the Smithsonian's research activities and its related efforts in conserving the 140 million or so objects and unique natural resources placed in its care. The resulting picture is but a snapshot; freeze the frame and new discoveries and new initiatives are excluded from view.

Because research goes on continually, no description of the Smithsonian's contributions can ever be complete. An exhaustive treatment would

A letter from President Andrew Jackson to Congress, forwarding papers related to the James Smithson bequest, echoed Smithson's desire to establish an institution for the "increase and diffusion of knowledge."

Heraldic symbols in the Smithsonian's ceremonial mace, created for the bicentennial of James Smithson's birth, reflect Smithson's life and work and the Institution's universal role. (Photo by Jeff Ploskonka)

be needed to account for the Institution's role as a major resource for thousands of scholars and scientists from other organizations. Each year, for example, the Smithsonian awards fellowships and grants to about 800 scholars and students, who use the Institution's unique resources in their research. Each year, more than 2,000 scientists visit the National Museum of Natural History to study its collections. An additional 2,000 researchers use the comprehensive data bases at the National Museum of American Art. More than 5,000 requests for public information on Asian art are handled by the

Freer Gallery of Art and the Arthur M. Sackler Gallery, and more than 3,000 come to the five regional offices of the Archives of American Art, which also lends microfilm copies of its collections to institutions around the world.

The examples in this publication convey the breadth of the Smithsonian's research effort, the Institution's commitment to fostering study of its holdings by scholars from around the world and, most important, its dedication to communicating this knowledge worldwide to both the scholarly community and the general public.

Research Tradition: The Increase of Knowledge

Since its beginning in 1846, the Smithsonian has been an organization with eclectic interests. Joseph Henry, the Institution's first secretary and one of the nation's pre-eminent scientists, sought to establish the Smithsonian chiefly as a center for research. The fledgling Institution supported studies in a variety of scientific fields, and it also served as the first home of the National Academy of Sciences, formed by Congress in 1863. Henry served as the scientific organization's second president.

Only grudgingly did the first secretary accept the Institution's congressionally designated role as the steward of the nation's collections of scientific and historical objects. Yet it was under Henry that the Smithsonian began its tradition of sponsoring research-and-collecting expeditions to such places as Alaska and the American Southwest, and it was Henry who hired as his assistant a young biologist named Spencer Fullerton Baird. With its new assistant secretary, the Smithsonian also received Baird's personal collection of natural history specimens—two railroad freight cars filled with bird skins, eggs, nests and other items. Baird's specimens were a healthy addition to the young Institution's own collections, primarily objects gathered during U.S. government-sponsored exploring expeditions.

Before the end of its first decade, the Smithsonian acquired its dual role and complex personality as both a research institution and a museum that weds increase of knowledge to its diffusion. History has proven the match a good one (see "College of Discoverers," Page 12). The collections are grist for the studies of Smithsonian researchers and the foundation for museum exhibitions. Like many-faceted gems, the objects in the Smithsonian's collections are examined and re-examined. Such repeated scrutiny is rewarded with added appreciation and understanding. New technology and methods of analysis, when wielded by researchers posing new questions about the past, the natural world, human cultures or any other subject that can be addressed through the collections, mine previously overlooked lodes of information. Far from being just a mammoth aggregation of relics, the Smithsonian's specimens and artifacts are dynamic research tools that, as one historian says, excite "three-dimensional thinking." Thus, it is not unusual to hear Smithsonian scholars confess that they are still learning how to use the collections—how to extract every bit of information from an object.

Henry's imprint—his guiding steps to fashion

the Smithsonian into a world-class research organization—persists in activities that go beyond studies of the collections. As a result, the strict definition of a museum—"a place in which works of artistic, historical and scientific value are cared for and exhibited"—does not do justice to the Smithsonian.

Through many activities, the Smithsonian participates in the ancient quest to understand our universe, our world and ourselves. These overall interests shape the Institution's research mission. Though research is pursued on many fronts—and in more than 150 countries—the boundaries that once formed separate provinces of understanding are merging. Increasingly, Smithsonian scholars work in teams, learn the tools of each others' disciplines and join with outside collaborators to craft multidisciplinary approaches to the exploration of complex problems and issues.

In the pages to come, join Smithsonian researchers in a world of discovery as they seek to expand the frontiers of knowledge in the sciences, the arts and history.

This portrait of James Smithson shows the Smithsonian founder as an Oxford student in the 1780s.

"COLLEGE OF DISCOVERERS"

"We have scarcely as yet read more than the title page and preface of the great volume of nature, and what we do know is nothing in comparison with that which may be yet unfolded and applied. . . ."—Joseph Henry, first secretary of the Smithsonian Institution

The Smithsonian's first secretary envisioned the Institution as a "college of discoverers" whose interests would span the applied and pure sciences. Even as he worked to build the new national organization, Henry made sure that it contributed to writing the "great volume of nature."

One installment was the *Ancient Monuments of the Mississippi Valley,* a study of Indian mounds published only two years after the Institution was established. That publication—followed by a report on the newly discovered planet Neptune—was the first in the Institution's first series, Smithsonian Contributions to Knowledge. At the time, the Smithsonian was one of only three U.S. institutions that sponsored the publication of research results. The series continues to this day, serving scholars worldwide.

Capitalizing on the nation's new telegraph system, Henry also set up a network of more than 200 weather observers, some located as far away as Bermuda, South America and Canada. By 1857, the Smithsonian was producing weather reports for much of the eastern half of the United States. The reports were first published in the Washington Evening Star. Building on this foundation, the government created the U.S. Weather Bureau in 1869.

Throughout its history, the Smithsonian has forged productive relationships with volunteer observers, and all of science has benefited. Henry's successor, Spencer Fullerton Baird, assembled a global network of more than 1,000 professional and amateur scientists to make collections of natural history specimens and Native American artifacts for the Smithsonian. Many decades later, on the eve of the Space Age and even before the launch of Sputnik 1, Fred Lawrence Whipple, then director of the Smithsonian As-

trophysical Observatory, enlisted teams of volunteer observers to assist in tracking artificial satellites. Today, the Smithsonian's Global Volcanism Network monitors volcanic activity, earthquakes and other geophysical phenomena with the aid of volunteer correspondents worldwide.

Motivated by scientific interests, the Smithsonian also contributed to exploration of the American frontier and Alaska. The Institution trained and outfitted many government-sponsored expeditions and, in return, received collections of minerals, rocks, soils, fossils and archaeological, anthropological, zoological and botanical specimens. Smithsonian naturalists accompanied an expedition to Alaska in the mid-1860s. The wealth of information they gathered is credited with influencing Congress' decision to purchase the territory from Russia.

Specimens gathered by these early expeditions continue to be used in research and exhibition programs on the natural and cultural histories of the Arctic. Indeed, the cultural artifacts and natural history specimens collected throughout the Smithsonian's long life have benefited science and society in numerous and often unforeseen ways. During the late 1960s, for example, scientists turned to the Institution's comprehensive collection of North American bird eggs, amassed during the 19th century. Comparisons showed that birds exposed to the pesticide DDT and other chemicals produced eggs with much thinner shells, often resulting in reproductive failure and population decline.

Among many other research accomplishments with lasting significance are the contributions of the Bureau of American Ethnology, the predecessor of today's Department of Anthropology and its National Anthropological Archives. The bureau was established in 1879 un-

der the leadership of John Wesley Powell, whose expedition to the uncharted Colorado River region had made him a national hero. The bureau's researchers—convinced that American Indian cultures were on the brink of destruction—hurried to document their languages, legends and customs.

Anthropologist Claude Levi-Strauss has described the bureau's studies and bountiful collection of photographs, documents, field notes and sound recordings as a "living inspiration," one of the Smithsonian's "greatest achievements."

Though sprinkled with heavy doses of experimentation—a willingness to tread new paths of inquiry—many of today's research efforts can trace their roots to the Institution's earlier years. For example, the National Zoological Park, which celebrated its centennial in 1989, arose largely from the desire of naturalist William T. Hornaday and the third Smithsonian secretary, Samuel Pierpont Langley, "to breed and replenish" the population of American bison. Now involved in breeding and conservation efforts around the world, the National Zoo was the first zoo dedicated to the preservation of threatened animals.

Most visitors to the Institution are not familiar with the Smithsonian Astrophysical Observatory, one of the world's major centers for astronomical research. Yet the Smithsonian has a century-long tradition of heavenly research. Fascinated by the sun's influence on the Earth's weather, Secretary Langley founded the observatory in 1890. He then established a major, long-term effort to quantify the "solar constant," a measure of the amount of radiation generated by the sun. Secretary Langley was also a pioneering investigator of mechanically powered flight. Smithsonian research support sustained both Langley's experiments and the early work of rocket pioneer Robert H. Goddard. ✳

John Wesley Powell, the first white man to descend the Colorado River, is shown here, in 1873, with Chief Taugu of the Paiutes in Utah, one of the many American Indians whom Powell encountered in the explorations that made him a national hero. (Photo by John K. Hillers)

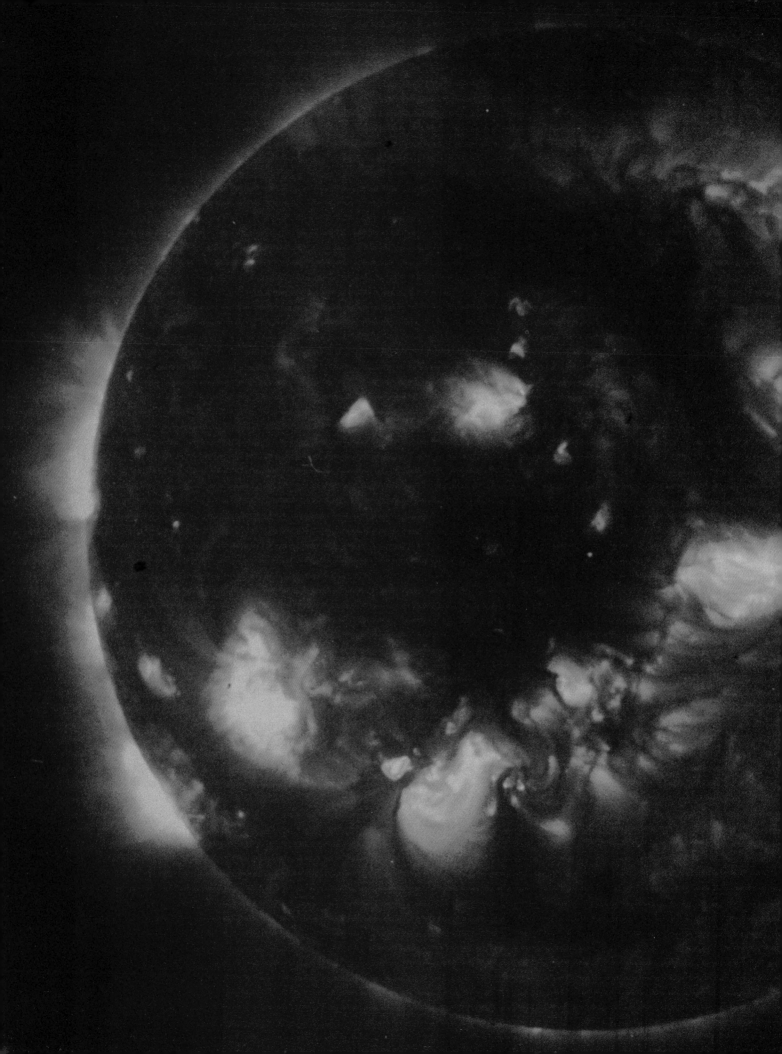

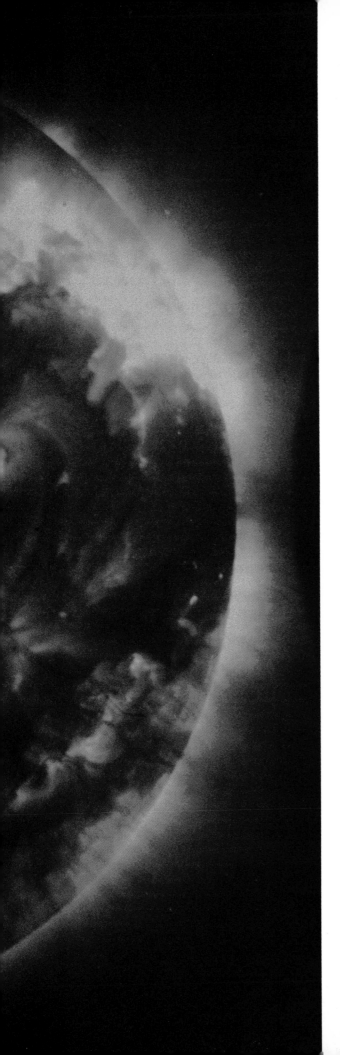

OUT
OF THIS
WORLD

A Look at Other Worlds from Earth
and at Earth from Outer Space

A Smithsonian Astrophysical Observatory-IBM rocket-borne telescope made this extremely high resolution X-ray photograph of the sun's hot outer atmosphere, or corona, as a total solar eclipse of the sun began in July 1991. The dark silhouette of the moon can be seen at the right. This unique image will contribute to a detailed three-dimensional model of the solar corona.

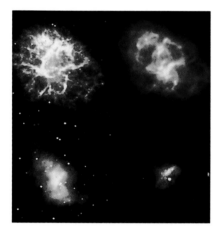

Four images of the Crab Nebula in (clockwise from upper left) optical (red light), radio, X-ray and optical (white light) emission. This object is the remnant of a supernova, or exploded star, whose outer shell of gas and dust continues to expand into space.

Studies of the heavens have humbled, inspired and mystified. Starting with Copernicus, who determined in the 16th century that the Earth revolves around the sun, astronomers slowly reversed the age-old belief that the sun and the planets reside at the center of a relatively compact universe. Today, we know that the solar system is but a tiny outpost near the outer edge of the Milky Way, which is, in turn, a rather unremarkable galaxy among about 100 billion galaxies in a universe of unfathomable dimensions.

But if we humans seem insignificant in the universe as a result of astronomical research, so, too, should we feel exhilarated by astronomers' findings that we — and all that we see and touch — are the indirect descendants of the stars. In the 1950s, scientists explained that most of the chemical elements in the universe were produced in the searing furnaces of stars and widely distributed through space by supernova explosions.

Almost always, new knowledge gained from astronomy and astrophysics research surprises as much as it clarifies. Or, as Alice in Wonderland said, it just gets "curiouser and curiouser." Mystery upon mystery remains to be solved. At the Smithsonian, researchers are looking at the mysteries of our universe.

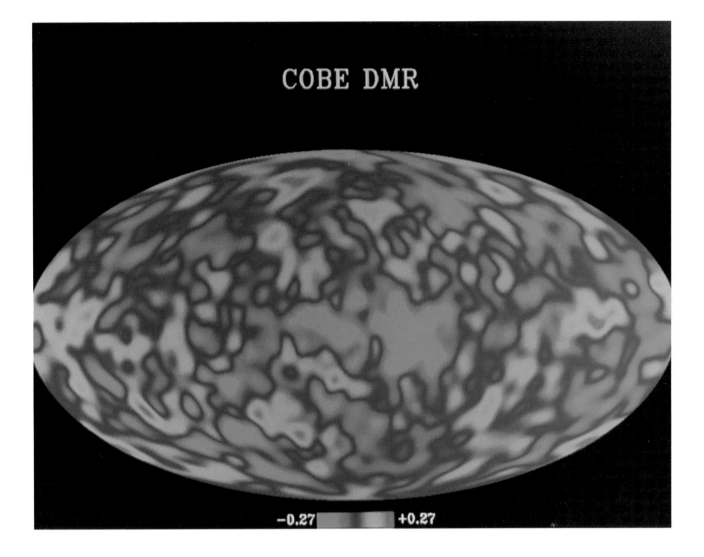

COBE DMR

−0.27   +0.27

The Early Universe

At the Harvard-Smithsonian Center for Astrophysics in Cambridge, Mass., one of the world's largest such facilities, astronomers, astrophysicists, atomic and molecular physicists, geophysicists and theorists study the universe with ground-based telescopes, manned and unmanned spacecraft, laboratory experiments, computers, and paper and pencils. Not only have the discoveries of Center scientists deepened and broadened our understanding of the universe, but their pioneering development of innovative methods and instruments—especially in X-ray, optical and radio astronomy—have opened new avenues of study.

The "Big Bang"

A logical place to begin exploring the Center's activities is with researchers studying the beginning of time itself, the tumultuous event that gave birth to the universe billions of years ago. At the instant of the big bang, most scientists agree, an infinitesimally small and dense point of pure energy "exploded." Over time, as the shell of the explosion fanned outward, matter and the physical forces that govern the universe began to take form.

The general outlines of the standard big-bang model of the universe are supported by observations and experiments. But the model glosses over other important matters. Clumps of stars in galaxies and the clustering of galaxies appear to result from gravitational instabilities in the early universe. But the big-bang model does not explain how these instabilities arose. Rather, the model assumes that slight variations in the density of matter, which caused the gravitational field to vary, existed from the outset.

Disturbed by the model's failure to account for a mechanism that steered the universe into today's observed state, former Center theorist Alan

This microwave map of the whole sky was made from data taken by NASA's Cosmic Background Explorer spacecraft. Predictions from the "inflationary big-bang" theory were supported by computer analysis of the temperature variations (color-coded in the map) found in the relic cosmic microwave background radiation.

Guth proposed a revolutionary idea. Using the complex but elegant language of mathematics, Guth suggested that the early universe underwent a bizarre inflationary period. Although measured in exceedingly small fractions of a millionth of a second, this tremendous burst of expansion persisted over a relatively long time span in terms of the age of the universe at that time. Doubling in size about every billionth of a trillionth of a trillionth of a second, the universe had grown enormously after just one-millionth of a second. By then, the theory explains, the inflationary phase had endowed the universe with many of its current properties.

The concept of an inflationary universe has been refined by other theorists since Guth's announcement in 1981, but it remains speculative, a general picture of how the universe might have evolved. The theory's predictions must be tested, a task that will take many years. One of its predictions, that small variations in the density from place to place were laid down during the inflationary period at the origin of the universe, has been verified by the National Aeronautics and Space Administration's Cosmic Background Explorer spacecraft, which found small variations in temperatures over the sky (see figure on Page 17).

Outside the Milky Way

Theorists rely heavily on results of experiments, providing them with data to refine their ideas. In turn, predictions derived from theories guide the directions of experimental and observational research. Results may support or disprove a theory or, as is often the case in astronomy, they may baffle, presenting theorists with the task of explaining phenomena that stretch the conceptual limits of the human mind.

The "Bubble Universe"

Center astronomers caused considerable head-scratching when they presented their observations of the large-scale structure of the universe. According to the "cosmological principle," one of the basic tenets of astronomy, the universe should look the same in all directions, at least when viewed on scales of several hundred million light-years (light travels about 6 trillion miles in one year). But John Huchra, Margaret Geller and Valerie de Lapparent did not find such uniformity. Rather, their still-growing map of galaxies within about 300 million light-years of Earth indicates that the universe is permeated by voids surrounded by sheetlike clusters of galaxies. The scientists liken the pattern to soap bubbles. The galaxies are akin to the filmy surfaces of the bubbles; the voids of seemingly empty space correspond to bubbles' interiors.

These voids are enormous, some measuring at least 150 million light-years across. But as the mapping has expanded, the researchers have found even larger structures, filling the very reaches of the survey itself. For example, a "great wall" of galaxies, perhaps representing a chain of bubble surface intersections, stretches a half-billion light-years across their map. The size of the walls and voids seem to defy explanation by any current models for large-scale structure. Gravity alone could not move matter from the voids and foster formation of galaxies along their borders on the time scale available for evolution. Of course, the voids may not really be empty, but rather filled with "dark" matter invisible to viewing instruments.

New Images of the Universe

Surprises often follow new ways of seeing into space. Until recently, visible light—that portion of the spectrum human eyes can see—provided the sole means of observing the night sky. Visible light remains a productive source of information, especially with advanced telescopes (see "Innovations on an Arizona Mountaintop," Page 25). But limiting observations to visible light is similar to being served a grand, seven-course meal and eating only the bread because no utensils are provided. Not to be deprived of nourishment, astronomers and astrophysicists have learned to use new instruments for studying the cosmos, often building the equipment themselves.

The Center for Astrophysics has been a leader in developing methods for viewing the universe in all portions of the electromagnetic spectrum (see "Reading the Light," Page 28). With methods and instruments for detecting radiation in the radio, infrared, ultraviolet, X-ray and gamma-ray portions of the spectrum, new windows on the universe have been opened. The new vision has revealed a cosmos that is not serene and stable, unchanging and everlasting, but rather dynamic, evolving and often violent, populated by energetic quasars and pulsars, powerful black holes, seething clouds of gas and other exotic objects.

Discoveries made with the National Aeronautics and Space Administration's High Energy Astronomy Observatory-2 satellite, better known as the "Einstein Observatory," illustrate just how re-

"To put in conjunction the words Harvard and Smithsonian ... is to designate not a place nor an assemblage of equipment, but rather a kind of astronomical personality. The two names belong together, certainly."—H.T. Kirby-Smith, *in* U.S. Observatories: A Directory and Travel Guide, *Van Nostrand and Reinhold (1976)*

The Smithsonian part of this astronomical personality—the Smithsonian Astrophysical Observatory—was established in 1890 by Samuel Pierpont Langley, the Institution's third secretary. SAO was a pioneer in research on the sun and the interrelationship between solar and terrestrial phenomena, concentrating almost exclusively on these subjects for more than half a century.

Studies by Charles Greeley Abbot, who succeeded Langley as SAO director and later became the Smithsonian's fifth secretary, resulted in the first estimates of the solar constant, a measure of total incoming solar radiation falling on the Earth. Although SAO had modest headquarters on the National Mall in Washington, D.C., the solar radiation studies were conducted at observatories set up in desolate locations chosen primarily for their high percentage of sunny days.

During the 1940s and early 1950s, SAO's research program flagged, only to be reinvigorated in 1955 with the appointment of Harvard astronomer Fred L. Whipple as director. The observatory moved from Washington to the grounds of the Harvard College Observatory in Cambridge, Mass. SAO began to flourish almost immediately. One of Whipple's first acts was to set up an international satellite-tracking network to aid research carried out as part of the International Geophysical Year of 1957–1958. By the mid-1960s, SAO's research program had grown in tandem with the nation's young space program, and its staff increased to nearly 500 employees. In 1967, SAO began construction of a multipurpose observatory on Mount Hopkins, in Amado, Ariz. Now named the Whipple Observatory, in honor of SAO's former director, it ranks among the world's top astronomical fa-

cilities, and it is the site of the Multiple Mirror Telescope, operated jointly with the University of Arizona.

Increasingly close ties between SAO and the Harvard College Observatory were formalized in 1973 with the formation of the Harvard-Smithsonian Center for Astrophysics. Research conducted by the some 200 Smithsonian and Harvard scientists under a single director, Irwin Shapiro, addresses nearly every major topic in modern astronomy. ✶

Charles Greeley Abbot, fifth secretary of the Institution and an avid solar energy proponent, with his demonstration solar energy collector, on the grounds of the Smithsonian Institution Building.

Scientists have an accounting problem of universal proportions. An enormous discrepancy shows up in every galaxy they study. In each, the total amount of visible matter is about 90 percent less than that needed to account for the gravitational forces directing the motions of stars and other identifiable objects. Where and what this "dark matter" is represent two of the most vexing questions facing researchers.

Two space-borne observatories, which are known as the Advanced X-ray Astrophysics Facility (AXAF I and s), promise to uncover important clues for solving this mystery when launched at the end of the decade. In fact, with the bounty of data AXAF I and s will gather during their anticipated five- to 10-year stays in space, scientists may be able to answer many perplexing problems in astronomy, from establishing the age of the universe to determining whether black holes truly exist.

Successor to the Einstein Observatory, which so greatly expanded understanding of the universe, AXAF will be 100 times more sensitive to X-ray emissions, produce images that are 10 times sharper, and offer other significant improvements in detection and imaging capabilities.

The Center's High Energy Astrophysics Division is playing a key role in AXAF development. A team, led by Stephen S. Murray, is responsible for designing AXAF-I's main instrument, a $30 million high-resolution imaging camera, and for building many of its components. Harvey Tananbaum and other division members are serving as advisers to NASA's Marshall Space Flight Center on scientific and engineering aspects of the entire AXAF project. In addition, Center scientists are developing the computer software that will be used to analyze AXAF data.

In March 1991, NASA announced its choice of the Smithsonian to plan, develop and operate the worldwide science support center for the AXAF observatories. The contract's value is approximately $75 million for the first 10-year period.

When fully developed, the science support center will receive, analyze and archive data from the AXAF observatories and function as a central clearinghouse of information and support for astronomers using the facilities. The science center, with about 100 scientific and technical personnel, will be based primarily in Cambridge.

The science center will also provide support during development of AXAF and its complement of sensitive instruments, for the testing and verification of ground support systems, for instrument calibration and for orbital operations that relate to the science instrument data. ✳

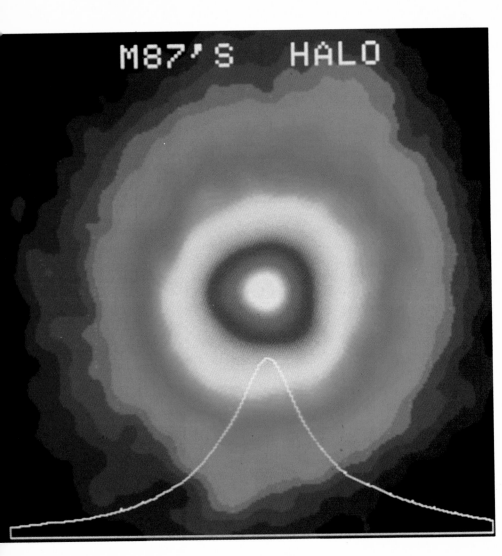

In this Einstein Observatory satellite image, a halo of hot, X-ray-emitting gas surrounding the giant elliptical galaxy M87, in the constellation Virgo, is shown by an intensity curve extending far beyond the bright central core.

The Whipple Observatory's 60-inch and 48-inch telescopes on Mount Hopkins, Ariz., are bracketed by two large optical reflectors used for gamma-ray astronomy, which includes confirmation of gamma-ray emission from the Crab Nebula and the first detection of ultra-high-energy radiation from another galaxy. (Photo by Mark Lawrence)

warding these new views can be. Before the observatory's launch in 1978, opportunities for viewing the X-ray universe were few. The Earth's atmosphere absorbs X-rays, so observations must be carried out in space. Expectations for Einstein, based on such previous, limited observations, indicated that the energetic processes required to produce X-rays exist in only a handful of exotic objects.

Almost as soon as the Einstein Observatory began transmitting images to researchers at the Center—who had designed and built two of the main instruments aboard the spacecraft—these expectations proved erroneous. The observatory, a thousand times more sensitive than previous X-ray instruments, revealed that the universe is ablaze in X-rays. In our galaxy alone, stars thought to be too cool or too inactive to be X-ray sources were found to be prolific emitters.

When Einstein's instruments were trained on objects outside the Milky Way, the discoveries were no less significant. X-ray images of other galaxies yielded insights into processes in our own galaxy. The brightest of these X-ray sources were distant, intensely energetic galaxies known as quasars. At the core of these quasars, according to one theory, lie supermassive black holes that gobble up nearby stars and gas, generating streams of X-rays in the process.

Studies of X-ray images now suggest that the Milky Way and other "older" galaxies began as quasars. Over the course of billions of years, the black hole thought to be at the center of the Milky Way may have consumed its fuel, reducing X-ray emissions from the galactic core.

Although the Einstein Observatory stopped working in 1981, after a longer-than-expected tour of duty, the more than 5,000 images it produced continue to be the source of discoveries. The Einstein Data Bank draws researchers from around the world to analyze X-ray-emitting objects on the Center's computers. To date, studies of the X-ray data have resulted in more than 1,000 scientific publications.

But as revealing as the Einstein mission was, it provided only a tantalizing sample of the knowledge to be gained from X-ray studies. Working with NASA and other organizations, Center scientists and engineers are designing and developing instruments for a new X-ray observatory. The planned Advanced X-ray Astrophysics Facility should push wide open the X-ray window on the universe (see "Advanced X-ray Astrophysics Facility," Page 20).

In and Around the Milky Way

Today, radio telescopes—saucer-shaped antennae that focus incoming radio waves onto detectors—investigate all portions of the universe. When used as interferometers, that is, two or more antennae linked for simultaneous observations, occasionally in networks spanning several continents, radio telescopes are capable of achieving high angular resolution of some of the most distant and unusual objects in the heavens.

The CfA's large team of radio astronomers has played a leading role in developing Very Long Baseline Interferometry, as the technique is called. CfA astronomers use VLBI to study the expansion of the universe, supernovae and the active centers of distant galaxies, including some suspected of harboring quasars.

Within the Milky Way, powerful objects called masers are a major interest of CfA radio astronomers. First discovered in the early 1960s, these cosmic microwave beacons are dense clouds of water, methanol or other molecules that are energized by the radiation processes of nearby stars. The influx of energy excites the electrons in the molecules, which then emit intense beams of microwaves, all of the same wavelength and all traveling in lockstep fashion. As a result, masers channel the original energy contribution of nearby stars and beam it outward like superpowerful radio transmitters.

Masers are often found in areas of star formation—gas-filled regions impervious to most means of observation—and they often occur in association with red giants and supergiants, stars past prime, having exhausted most of their hydrogen fuel. This means CfA radio astronomers can use the objects to study the birth and death of stars.

Masers also serve as precise distance markers for measuring the vast expanses in the universe. The Center's Mark J. Reid, Matthew H. Schneps, James M. Moran and Carl R. Gwinn, along with three European colleagues, used high-precision VLBI measurements of maser motions and complex statistical methods to calculate the distance to masers residing near the heart of the Milky Way. The effort yielded the most accurate estimate yet of the expanse between the sun and the galactic center. Their estimate of about 23,000 light-years places the sun about 4,500 light-years closer to the galactic center than the previously accepted measure. CfA astronomer David Latham and colleagues from the University of North Carolina, using visible-light measurements of globular-cluster stars in the Milky Way's halo, arrived at a comparable estimate of the sun's distance from the galactic center.

These measurements, which both teams are refining, will trigger revisions of other important astronomical benchmarks. For example, the "shortened" span between the sun and the galactic center decreases the distance between the Milky Way and its neighboring galaxies, and it reduces the total mass of the Milky Way.

Interstellar Chemistry

Once thought to be devoid of chemical activity, the regions between stars are now known to contain not only solitary atoms of hydrogen and helium—the bulk of the interstellar medium—but also a diverse array of molecules. The 80 or so molecules identified to date have revealed much about the process of star formation and the physical conditions within a galaxy. Moreover, the discovery of many "organic," or carbon-based, molecules supports speculation that the chemical building blocks of life on Earth originated in the cosmos.

One of these molecules, carbon monoxide, has served as a pathfinder in the Milky Way, leading astronomers to the galaxy's star-forming hot spots, where the gas emits microwave signals easily detected on Earth.

With two hard-working but disarmingly small radio telescopes (one perched on the roof of the Center's headquarters in Cambridge and the other located at an observatory in Chile), radio astronomers Patrick Thaddeus, Thomas Dame and their collaborators have mapped the distribution of carbon monoxide in the Milky Way. Microwave signals in our galaxy, in fact, exposed hundreds of giant clouds of molecules, which rank as the most massive objects in the Milky Way. Despite their enormous size—some measure a thousand light-years across and contain more gas than a million suns—the molecular clouds escape detection with other observing methods.

Tremendous size is not the clouds' most notable feature, however. Stars form deep within such clouds, as dramatically revealed in the maps prepared by Center researchers and their colleagues. These "stellar nurseries" reside in the Milky Way's spiral arms. Traced by carbon monoxide molecules, the majestic swirls and their branching arms appear to light up like strings of lights on a Christmas tree.

Inside the Solar System

About 5 billion years ago, the sun and the planets began to condense in a spinning, collapsing cloud of interstellar gas and dust, beginning an extraordinary series of events that included the emergence of life on Earth. To date, our solar system remains the sole source for study of planetary evolution.

The Sun

At the top of the list, perhaps, are questions about the sun, a middle-aged star that sustains life on Earth. The sun is the ultimate governor of the planet's weather and climate. Very little, however, is known about variations in this star's energy production and how such cyclic phenomena as sunspots and solar flares influence conditions on Earth. Also poorly understood are the mechanisms that heat the solar corona, the sun's outer atmosphere, to about 1.8 million degrees Fahrenheit—as compared with more than 7,000 F on the sun's surface—and that power the violent solar wind spewing out of this corona to swirl by the planets at speeds of about 1 million miles per hour. In fact, when the puzzle of the heating of the solar corona is solved, scientists will know a lot more about the workings of all stars, not just the sun.

Astrophysicists suspect that the tortuous fields of strong magnetic activity appearing and disappearing on the sun's surface are directly involved in heating the corona and driving the solar wind. Details are sketchy, however, because ground-based observations of the sun's outer atmosphere are limited to solar eclipses. Moreover, the corona is brightest in ultraviolet light, which is blocked by the Earth's atmosphere. To date, all the information on the corona's ultraviolet emissions has been assembled from a total of about 15 minutes of observations made during the short flights of sub-orbital rockets.

The paucity of data should end during the next few years. First, an ultraviolet coronagraph-spectrometer, built by a team of Center scientists and engineers led by John Kohl, is part of a scientific package awaiting launch, planned for spring 1993, by the space shuttle. The instrument will observe the corona for 40 hours.

A much broader scientific expedition scheduled for the mid-1990s should reveal even more. A satellite called the Solar and Heliospheric Observatory will be positioned a million miles above the Earth. Sitting directly in the path of the solar wind, SOHO's instruments, including the Center's coronagraph-spectrometer, will observe the sun continuously, probing the mechanism of coronal heating and charting the evolution of the solar wind.

Sallie Baliunas and other Center scientists take a different approach to studying the sun. They have been monitoring variations in the brightness and magnetic activity of approximately 1,000 sunlike stars at different stages of evolution. These variable stars—so named because their brightness fluctuates—have episodes of activity that correspond to our sun's 11-year sunspot cycle and other

This celestial map, prepared by scientists Margaret Geller (shown here) and John Huchra, spans 500 million light-years of space and shows how galaxies are apparently distributed in vast sheets surrounding giant, bubblelike voids (see Page 18). (Photo by Joe Wrinn)

phenomena. From measurements of young stars, the team hopes to be able to deduce the behavior of the sun during the first 1 or 2 billion years of the solar system, when fluctuations in the sun's brightness were probably more pronounced than today. The analysis should also yield insights into the mechanisms that control the sunspot cycle and, perhaps, the early climate on Earth.

Until recently, the Center's research agenda—measuring the properties of hundreds of stars, some nightly and others two or three times a week—would be considered overly ambitious, if not impossible. Measurements of fluctuations in stellar brightness seen over long periods simply consume too much telescope time, already a scarce commodity among astronomers.

Now, however, every clear night on Mount Hopkins, the Arizona home of the Smithsonian's Whipple Observatory, a small robot telescope known as an Automated Photoelectric Telescope dutifully measures the brightness of scores of stars as instructed by a computer. The results, recorded on floppy disks, are mailed to the astronomers in Cambridge.

In the Earth's Neighborhood

Like the Harvard-Smithsonian Center for Astrophysics, the Center for Earth and Planetary Studies at the National Air and Space Museum concentrates research efforts on the planets (including Earth) and the moon. Researchers at CEPS study satellite-gathered images of the planets and the moon to deci-

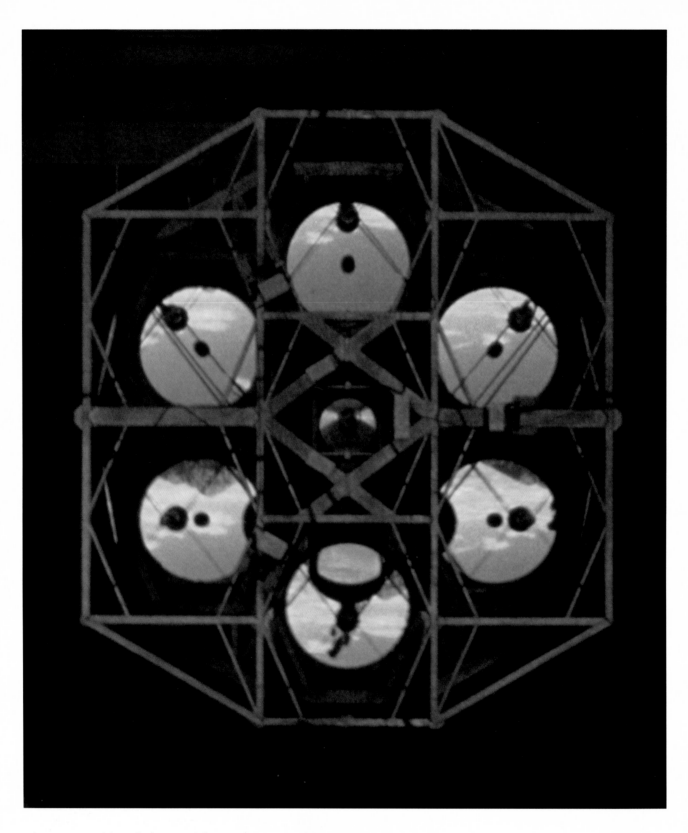

The six mirrors of the Multiple Mirror Telescope, a joint project of the Smithsonian Astrophysical Observatory and the University of Arizona, atop the 8,500-foot-high summit of Mount Hopkins in Arizona. (Photo by Gary Ladd)

Opposite: Ten tons of borosilicate glass are loaded into a mold for the 256-inch (6.5-meter) mirror, now successfully cast, that will replace the six mirrors of the Multiple Mirror Telescope. (Photo by Lori Stiles)

INNOVATIONS ON AN ARIZONA MOUNTAINTOP

Since it opened in 1968, the Smithsonian's observatory on Mount Hopkins in Arizona has been one of the world's most productive centers for ground-based astronomy. The facility owes much of this success to Smithsonian accomplishments in the design of new telescopes and light detectors, as well as development of computers for research.

From its half-mile-long ridge at the 7,600-foot-high level to its 8,550-foot summit, Mount Hopkins hosts an impressive and still-growing array of instruments to help unravel the mysteries of the universe. One such instrument—the Multiple Mirror Telescope—represents a radical and revolutionary departure from the design of conventional telescopes. The instrument combines six individual 72-inch reflecting telescopes in an array to produce the light-gathering capacity of a single 176-inch telescope. This made the MMT the world's third-largest optical telescope; yet it was compact and cost much less than a conventional single-mirror telescope of equivalent capacity.

Controlled by an extremely precise computer-directed alignment system, each telescope works in unison with the others, bringing the light received from celestial objects to a common focus. The MMT's success demonstrated that, with new technology, ground-based astronomy could overcome the so-called 200-inch size barrier, beyond which conventional telescopes in the past were technologically and financially impractical. The multiple-mirror concept has been adopted by other institutions that are developing even larger telescopes. This "new generation of telescopes" also benefits from other innovations introduced by the Smithsonian and the University of Arizona, including the use of altitude-azimuth mountings and housing in a co-rotating barnlike building.

Technology does not stand still, and now the MMT is slated for new radical changes. A spincasting technique pioneered at the University of Arizona makes it possible to break through the 200-inch barrier for a single mirror. And so, the MMT's six-mirror array is being exchanged for a single, relatively lightweight mirror about 256 inches in diameter. With this immense new telescope, researchers will be able to observe objects 2½ times fainter than those that can now be viewed with the MMT. They will also be able to study much larger sections of the sky, allowing simultaneous observation of many celestial objects. For example, with the hundredfold increase in the telescope's field of view, studies of clusters of galaxies, critical to understanding the distribution of matter in the universe and its large-scale structure, will require far less of the precious observing time. ✳

pher their geological histories. As a NASA-designated archives for planetary photographs and images taken by U.S. spacecraft, CEPS maintains more than 250,000 such items in its collection.

Mars, the target of a proposed manned mission in the 21st century, is a major interest of CEPS researchers. The red planet is a study of contrasts. Its northern hemisphere includes vast, smooth lowlands, some covered by lava from relatively recent volcanic activity, while the older, elevated terrain of the southern hemisphere is pocked by numerous impact craters. Scientists do not know how these marked differences in the planet's topography were formed.

CEPS scientists are actively involved in a geologic mapping program of Mars sponsored by NASA, in support of the selection of future landing sites for either unmanned or manned spacecraft. CEPS researchers Robert A. Craddock, Ted A. Maxwell, Thomas R. Watters and James R. Zimbelman are among the 20 principal investigators in the mapping program, producing geologic maps at 1:500,000 scale of ancient river channels, ridged plains, giant volcanoes and the landing area of the Viking I spacecraft. Eventually, all of the geologic maps will be published by the U.S. Geologic Survey as part of its on-going cartographic activities.

Tectonic features on the moon, Mars, Mercury and Venus are being studied to determine their origin and implications for the tectonic evolution of planetary surfaces. Studies by Watters involve the analysis of analog structures on the Earth, in particular in the continental flood-basalts of the Columbia Plateau in the northwestern United States. Kinematic and mechanical models developed for the origin of structures on the plateau are applied to tectonic features on the other terrestrial planets.

Studies of the Earth, both from the perspective of orbiting spacecraft and from the ground, are an important part of CEPS studies related to the problem of "global change." CEPS has an on-going program of studies in arid environments such as the desert areas of Africa and North America, providing a foundation for evaluating conditions brought on by changes in Earth's climate. CEPS researchers Maxwell, Zimbelman and Patricia A. Jacobberger utilize remote sensing and field data from arid and semi-arid regions to study growth of and changes in desert conditions, and Watters is working with scientists in the Czech Republic and at the University of New Hampshire to assess the loss of woodlands in the Czech Republic and elsewhere in eastern Europe.

The Moon

Before the U.S. space program put a man on the moon, speculation about the surface of Earth's satellite abounded. One theory held that the "seas," or marias, seen from Earth were awash in electrostatic dust particles that flowed like a liquid. When the Eagle landed in the Sea of Tranquility on July 20, 1969, astronauts Buzz Aldrin and Neil Armstrong did find a thick layer of dust. But the dust had none of the proposed exotic properties.

The Apollo 11 crew returned to Earth with about 50 pounds of lunar rocks and dust, providing scientists with an unprecedented opportunity to study the moon's surface. Geologist John A. Wood of the Center for Astrophysics was one of a handful of researchers chosen to receive a sample—10 grams in all—of this extraordinary treasure. Wood and other scientists soon discovered that the most notable characteristic of the lunar material was its similarity to rocks and dust on Earth. The moon's crust could be explained in terms of the same geological and mineralogical principles as the Earth's surface.

"This seems a trivial observation," Wood later wrote, "yet it illustrates what may have been the most profound lesson Apollo taught us: We had exaggerated the potential 'weirdness' of other bodies in the solar system."

Researchers at the National Museum of Natural History were also among the scientists who studied the lunar materials brought back on the six Apollo missions. In all, they identified more than

Studies of Mars, including the production of maps that will be used in the selection of future landing sites, involve the work of Tom Watters (left) and Bob Craddock, geologists at the Air and Space Museum's Center for Earth and Planetary Studies. (Photo by Carolyn Russo)

THE SMITHSONIAN INSTITUTION: A WORLD OF DISCOVERY

20 minerals, including one—an iron calcium silicate—not found on Earth. Scientists at this museum also identified the first meteorite collected from the moon.

Studies conducted by Smithsonian scientists have enhanced understanding of how various geological forces and events, especially the heavy bombardment by meteorites, combined to shape the moon's crust and dictate the composition of its rocks. And even though nearly 20 years have passed since the last Apollo mission, research on lunar samples continues to uncover new information about the moon.

Recently, CfA geologist Ursula Marvin and her colleagues identified a new mineral in a rock sample gathered by Apollo 15 astronauts. Called cordierite, the pinkish, magnesium-rich mineral is significant because it appears to have been formed under high-pressure conditions found between 16 and 30 miles below the lunar surface. In contrast, all the other lunar samples studied thus far either formed near the surface or only slightly deeper in the lunar crust. The scientists suggest that the rock sample—a white glass with two red crystals—was probably excavated by the impact of a meteorite collision that formed the moon's Imbrium Basin, where the sample was collected. With their discovery of a completely new rock type on the moon, Marvin and her associates provide a glimpse of a previously unstudied layer of the lunar crust.

Comets

Scientists often have to contend with skepticism when they propose new theories. Such was the case when Fred L. Whipple of the Center for Astrophysics proposed a novel answer to a solar system enigma. In 1950, Whipple, then a Harvard professor, hypothesized that the nuclei of comets are "dirty snowballs," loosely packed conglomerates of ice, rock and dust. The theory explained many features of comets, including their sometimes erratic orbits. The sun's heat vaporizes the ice in a comet, creating gas jets that may cause the comet to deviate somewhat from the path set by solar gravity.

Whipple's ideas became widely accepted, even before they were rigorously tested during the 1986 return of Halley's comet. On the comet's 28th known journey across the Earth's sky, a fleet of satellites was waiting. One of the five probes, the European satellite Giotto, flew to within 375 miles of the nucleus, and its detailed measurements confirmed the essential features of Whipple's "dirty snowball" model.

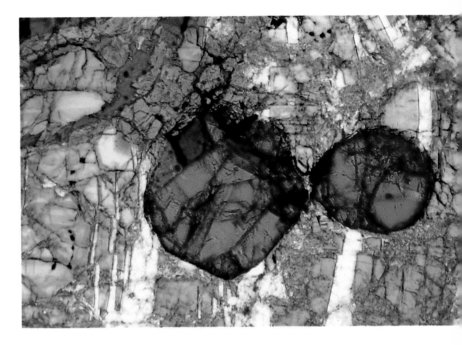

Comets are much more than eye-catching wanderers in the night sky. The quest to learn more about them is motivated by what their contents can reveal about the conditions that existed when the solar system was formed. Among the smallest objects in the solar system, comets are thought to reside in the Oort Cloud, a broad zone completely circling the solar system at a distance some two light-years from the sun. In this distant, frigid region, the cosmic past is preserved in these frozen objects, unaffected by other processes triggered by the formation of the solar nebula.

Asteroids and Meteorites

Clues to the origins of the solar system are also locked in asteroids, less visually spectacular pieces of cosmic debris. Millions of asteroids occupy a broad belt between the orbits of Mars and Jupiter and range from irregular, Manhattan-sized boulders to small chunks the size of rocks, gravel and sand. Unlike the clumps of primordial material that accumulated to become planets, the asteroids, for unknown reasons, did not coalesce. Perhaps, as Whipple has suggested, they are the leftover building materials of the solar system.

In the International Astronomical Union's Minor Planet Center, at CfA headquarters, Brian Marsden and his colleagues keep tabs on the thousands of asteroids observable from Earth. From more than 50,000 observations reported, some 4,000 asteroids have been named and their orbits precisely determined. Each year, the MPC issues

A fragment of lunar cordierite-spinel troctolite from the Apollo 15 mission. The cordierite, unknown prior to that mission, shows as lavender pink (upper left) in this color-enhanced image. (Photomicrograph by Ursula Marvin)

about 1,200 circulars advising astronomers on the orbits of asteroids coming into view, discoveries of new minor planets and recoveries of "lost" bodies—previously identified asteroids that have eluded subsequent observations.

Among the scientists who consult MPC circulars are those who study meteorites, the remnants of asteroid collisions. If they are lucky, finders of meteorites can match materials recovered on Earth with the parent asteroid in space.

Although most wayward objects from the asteroid belt burn up during descent through the Earth's atmosphere (in which case, they are known as meteors), a surprising amount of material—about 100,000 tons annually, according to one estimate—survives the journey, mostly as a fine rain of dust particles. Several thousand more substantial meteorites have been found on Earth, and craters carved out by the impacts of massive meteorites are scattered about the Earth's surface.

Although not the most convenient special-delivery system for getting information about conditions in the early solar system, meteorites are the closest thing to a firsthand account. And some meteorites, the rare "carbonaceous chondrites," bring clues to phenomena outside the solar system, for they may contain traces of matter expelled by stars and supernovae.

The One and Only Solar System?

Nobel Prize-winning physicist Enrico Fermi posed the question succinctly. Pondering the prospects for life elsewhere in the universe, he asked, "Where is everybody?"

Where, indeed? Many experts say it is logical to assume that our planet is not the only repository of life in the vast universe or even in our own spacious galaxy. The formation of a planetary system, which most scientists believe is a necessary condition for the emergence and evolution of lifeforms, is not likely to be a one-time event. That years of searching have not yielded definitive evidence of other planetary systems probably reflects more the difficulty of the task and the limitations of observing instruments than the uniqueness of the solar system.

A Promising Candidate

Center for Astrophysics astronomers and an outside collaborator recently found strong evidence of a planet orbiting a star when they discovered a slight wobble in the motion of a star about 90 light-years from Earth. The wobble in the orbit of star HD 114762 is caused by the gravitational tugging of a low-mass companion, which the researchers believe is a giant planet some 10 to 20

READING THE LIGHT

Current knowledge of the composition and workings of stars, planets, interstellar clouds of gas and dust, and other celestial objects has been gleaned from light-encoded packets of data called spectra, astronomy's counterpart to fingerprints.

That so much has been learned from series of lines recorded on photographic plates and by electronic detectors is one of the great success stories of astronomy. At the Center for Astrophysics, an entire division is devoted to deciphering the complex atomic and molecular processes that create light in, say, a star and then alter this light before it reaches a telescope on Earth or in space.

A star emits a characteristic spectrum, or pattern, of electromagnetic radiation that reflects its chemical composition, temperature and direction of movement. If the body is extremely hot, most of the radiation will be in the form of ultraviolet rays, X-rays and gamma rays. The lower-energy light from cooler bodies will have longer wavelengths, characteristic of visible light, infrared light and radio waves. On its journey through space, however, the starlight must pass through clouds of gas and dust. During the encounter, the intervening material may absorb some of the incoming radiation or amplify it.

Thus, the star's original fingerprint is transformed into a hybrid composition that contains some information about the stellar body and some information about the materials encountered by the starlight.

To make sense out of this complicated situation, scientists in the Atomic and Molecular Physics Division often try to reproduce the chemistry of space in the lab. They search for the types of atoms and molecules, and the relative abundance of each, that combine to produce a specific set of spectral lines. In tandem with laboratory studies, they develop theories that can explain basic physical processes. Thus, many of the mysteries of the vast universe can be solved only by understanding events that occur on scales measured in hundred-millionths of a centimeter. ✸

times more massive than Jupiter. Astronomers working at an observatory in southern France confirmed the finding, but more analyses are needed to determine that the object is indeed a planet.

Unfortunately, the astronomers cannot image the companion object directly, a feat that would be comparable to distinguishing the light of a single candle standing beside a powerful searchlight on the surface of the moon. Because of the extreme faintness of planets, those suspected to exist outside the solar system must be sought through indirect means. Thus, Center astronomers look for subtle changes in the light emitted by stars. From these changes, the researchers can ascertain whether the star is periodically pulled away from or toward the Earth, signaling a shift in velocity caused by the gravitational attraction of a nearby object. The star HD 114762 provides the best evidence to date for having a planetary companion.

The discoverers of HD 114762 continue to search for other stars that may have planetary companions, using the 61-inch reflecting telescope at the Smithsonian-operated Oak Ridge Observatory in Massachusetts. HD 114762 also remains under scrutiny—to learn more about its companion and to determine whether more planets might be lurking nearby.

New Tools

New observing instruments could aid the hunt for primeval planetary systems. At the Smithsonian's Whipple Observatory, for example, scientists and engineers are building an Infrared-Optical Telescope Array. The new instrument, being developed by the Smithsonian and four other institutions, will capitalize on the interferometry technique developed by radio astronomers—the use of two or more antennae to observe the same object simultaneously, resulting in high-resolution images. Project IOTA will use this method to observe objects in the optical and infrared wavebands. With two small telescopes separated by up to 165 feet, the resulting resolution will be equivalent to that of a single telescope with a 165-foot lens, about 10 times the size of today's largest optical telescopes.

Now in the construction phase is another Smithsonian-conceived observing system, an array of six "submillimeter" telescopes. Lying on the electromagnetic spectrum between the radio and infrared bands, submillimeter radiation provides another means of penetrating the gas- and dust-shrouded sites of star formation. This unique instrument, capable of producing images with a resolution comparable to the best optical telescopes, will probe a largely unexplored region of the spectrum.

Artist's conception of the Submillimeter Wave Astronomy Satellite, to be launched later this decade. The SWAS is being planned by astronomers at the Center for Astrophysics and the National Air and Space Museum to study submillimeter radiation from space. (Ball Aerospace Systems Group illustration)

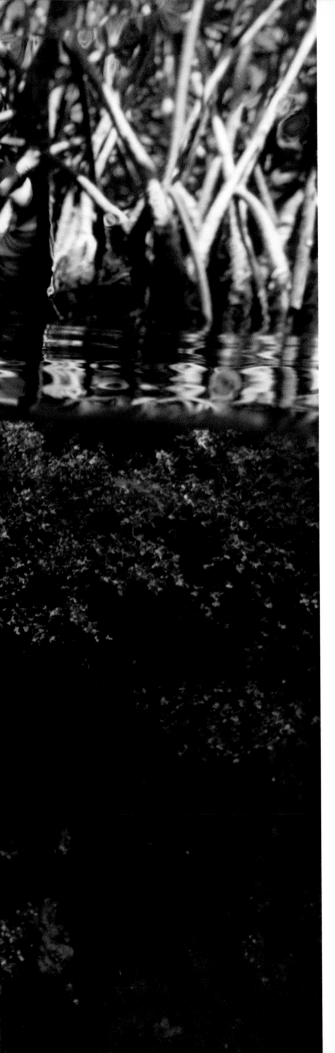

DOWN

TO

EARTH

A Journey from the Highest
Mountains to the Deepest Oceans
with Smithsonian Scientists

*This mangrove coast in Belize, typical of those found throughout
the tropics, reveals an ecosystem below the water line as complex
as that above, providing a fertile site for multidisciplinary studies.
(Photo by Chip Clark)*

This unusually well-preserved tektite from Australia measures 1 inch from side to side. These curious forms, produced by the impact of a very large meteorite with the surface of the Earth some 780,000 years ago, were scattered across 10 percent of the globe. (Photo by Vic Krantz)

The story of the Earth's past is a story of suspense, full of intertwined subplots revolving around the unexpected twists and turns in the lives of an ever-changing cast of characters in an ever-changing landscape. The planet's present is also the stuff of drama, taut with the tension of environmental uncertainties. The account of the Earth's future remains to be written, although the details are the products of today's decisions. Whether the unfolding tale will be a tragedy or a success story depends on whether we understand the past and on how we use that understanding in the present.

Smithsonian researchers are involved in writing each of these stories. The current account of the Earth's natural history, a story that spans billions of years, is far from complete. How has the shuffling of the continental plates shaped and reshaped the Earth's surface? How did the first life forms evolve? What evolutionary forces have fostered the stunning diversity of life in the tropics and the complex relationships among the species that live there? What events conspired to cause wholesale extinctions at various points in the planet's past? These are only a few of the questions that motivate the pursuits of the Smithsonian's geologists and biologists.

Many of the 200 scientists at the National Museum of Natural History and at affiliated federal agencies working in that museum are trying to trace the evolutionary relationships that link all plants and animals, living and extinct. The picture emerging from these efforts reveals the natural world as an interdependent, coherent whole. The damaging toll of habitat loss, pollution and other environmental ills is not confined to the ecosystems immediately affected. Rather, the consequences can spread well beyond national boundaries.

Awareness has bred a sense of urgency, raising environmental and ecological problems to a place near the top of international concerns. Dozens of scientists at several Smithsonian bureaus are studying the most pressing of these issues: acid rain, global warming caused by the greenhouse effect, deterioration of the ozone layer, clear-cutting of tropical forests, desertification and pollution of the oceans.

Their studies of the Earth and its organisms are fact-finding missions. This basic research provides the information necessary for understanding the consequences of today's environmental problems and for crafting prudent responses. Without this underpinning, well-intended corrective measures are likely to fail or make matters worse.

On the Surface

Clues to the Earth's distant past are few. Geologists believe that the Earth, like the rest of the solar system, formed about 4.6 billion years ago. Yet the oldest rocks exhumed from the Earth's crust are about 3.8 billion years old, resulting in an 800-million-year gap in the geologic record. And because the Earth's surface is constantly refashioning itself, materials older than 600 million years have become increasingly scarce. In fact, rocks on the ocean floor are less than 200 million years old.

Given the scarcity of information, geologists who have taken on the task of describing the planet's past must gather clues through a variety of methods. Some Smithsonian scientists study geophysical processes at work today—glaciation, erosion, volcanism, earthquakes and the movement of continental plates. Others conduct detailed X-ray studies of the structure and composition of rocks, piecing together information that reveals how the rocks were formed.

Extraterrestrial Clues

The Apollo missions provided tangible evidence that the moon's surface was pitted by a heavy rain of meteorites during its first several hundred million years. Scientists believe that the early Earth also weathered heavy meteorite bombardment, although the direct evidence of this theory is lacking.

Researchers speculate that the Earth's surface cooled much more slowly than the moon's. Meteorites dotted the moon's thick, rigid surface with impact craters. The Earth's thin crust, in contrast, could not withstand the assault. According to one theory, the meteorites penetrated deep into the Earth, perhaps creating irregularities in the mantle layer that eventually produced the growth of continents.

The rate of early encounters between the Earth and meteorites must be inferred from studies of the moon and neighboring planets, but some evidence of collisions is preserved in the terrestrial crust. Impact craters—about 200 in all—are scattered about the world. These range in diameter from tens of meters to the 120-mile Sudbury Basin in Ontario. Many, many more terrestrial impact craters must have once existed, only to be erased or obscured by the Earth's active crust and the erosive effects of wind and water.

The largest of these collisions probably had catastrophic consequences, repeatedly changing the course of life on Earth. For example, though their ideas are far from proven, some scientists propose that, about 65 million years ago, an enormous meteorite caused the extinction of the dinosaurs plus many other terrestrial and marine organisms, large and small. Supporting evidence for the theory is a thin global clay layer rich in the element iridium—rare on Earth but relatively abundant in

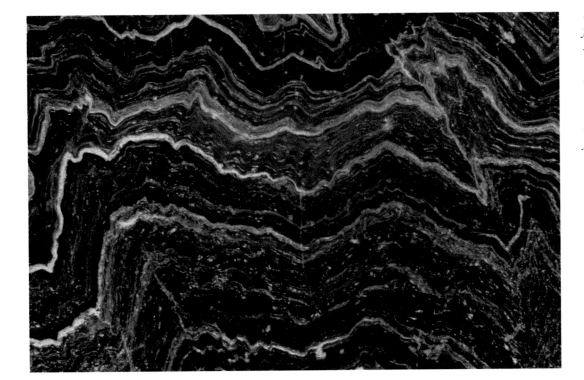

Rocks like this one from the Smithsonian collections were crumpled during plate collisions and reflect, on a small scale, the gigantic force that resulted in mountain building. (Photo by Vic Krantz)

meteorites—that corresponds to the time of the extinction. The theory's proponents suggest that the meteorite ejected mountains of dust into the air and triggered fires. A worldwide curtain of dust and soot plunged the Earth into cold and darkness, curtailing plant growth and disrupting the food chain.

Through his research on impact craters, Robert Fudali, a geologist at the Museum of Natural History, hopes to clarify the debate over the impact theory of extinction. Fudali and his colleagues are interested in re-creating the form of the craters at the time of impact, an analysis that can yield estimates of the energy released in the collision. Earlier work in an area known as the Australasian strewnfield—a region that extends from Madagascar to South China—suggests that the energy required to cause wholesale extinctions would be incredibly large. The strewnfield covers 12 percent of the globe and is apparently the legacy of a meteorite that struck the Earth some 780,000 years ago. Glassy, impact-created objects called tektites are scattered across this large region. The energy required to melt and disperse the estimated 100 million tons of glass over this region should have also created a crater at least 62 miles in diameter, but the remnants of such an enormous crater have not been found. This cataclysmic event, however, does correspond with a reversal of the Earth's mag-

netic field. Still, the meteorite that created the Australasian strewnfield is not associated with even minor extinctions.

Jigsaw Earth

In *Basin and Range,* his lyrical treatise on the "new geology," author John McPhee wrote that if he were forced to reduce his work to a single sentence, he would have chosen this one: "The summit of Mount Everest is marine limestone."

The strength of that sentence lies in its apparent incongruity. At the top of the world's highest peak, nearly six miles above sea level, are fossilized rocks that, millions of years ago, resided perhaps four miles below the sea floor! The rocks' 10-mile ascent is the result of a continental collision—between the Indian land mass and Asia. India both squeezed and plowed under Asia, creating the Himalayas and elevating the Tibetan plateau to its lofty perch.

Such is the power of the movements of the 20 large chunks of rigid terrestrial crust and upper mantle that slide atop the Earth's conveyor belt, its plastic lower mantle. Though the concept was proposed decades earlier, only in the 1960s did the theory of plate tectonics, sometimes called continental drift, gain acceptance. Researchers in the Department of Mineral Sciences at the Museum of Natural History have been instrumental in explaining

---

TRACKING PLATE MOVEMENTS

One of the biggest boons to research on crustal movements of the Earth is a contribution from radio astronomy: Very Long Baseline Interferometry, or VLBI. Center for Astrophysics Director Irwin Shapiro was one of the first scientists to recognize how the combination of widely separated radio telescopes and fixed reference points in space—quasars, enigmatic objects billions of light-years from the Earth—could be used to track crustal movements with high precision. By observing the same quasars simultaneously, the network of instruments can establish the position of each telescope relative to the others. From repeated measurements of the quasars, scientists can ascertain

changes in the telescopes' positions, a reflection of plate movement.

The CfA's radio observatory near Fort Davis, Texas, and others across the United States and around the world make cooperative measurements of plate movements and changes in the magnitude and directions of the Earth's spin. These measurements have demonstrated that the jigsaw pieces of the Earth's crust separated by the mid-Atlantic Ridge—the North American and Eurasian Plates—are now moving apart at the rate of about half an inch a year, while the Pacific Plate slides northward along the California coast at an annual rate of about 3 inches.

Also capitalizing on the fixed ref-

erence points near the edge of the universe, Shapiro and fellow CfA radio astronomers Carl R. Gwinn and Thomas A. Herring uncovered properties of the boundary between the Earth's liquid core and the solid mantle that lies above it. Their study was based on the VLBI measurements of unexpected annual changes in the orientation of the Earth's spin axis that are akin to the motions of an unsteady top. From these changes, the Center team inferred that this core-mantle boundary was about a third of a mile more out of round than had been previously thought. This difference is particularly important for understanding interactions between the Earth's core and the mantle. ✳

the geophysical consequences of the Earth's dynamic, jigsaw-puzzle construction. Smithsonian geologist William G. Melson was one of the chief scientists aboard the National Science Foundation's Glomar Challenger when the drilling ship extracted the first deep-crustal cores from the mid-Atlantic Ridge, a "mountain range" almost entirely beneath the ocean. At the center of the serpentlike ridge of submarine volcanoes that separates the North American and Eurasian plates, molten material from the Earth's interior rises to the ocean's bottom, pushing the plates further apart.

Melson and his Smithsonian colleagues continue to study the sites of sea-floor spreading and the Earth's subduction zones, where the crust plunges back down into the mantle. Their investigations include studies of how eons of continental pushing and pulling have shaped the crust. Research in the American West is helping to explain the region's complex and violent geological past, and it is sorting out the interacting forces that continue to deform the crust. For example, Smithsonian geologist Glenn MacPherson is trying to deduce the details of how one ancient subduction zone worked by studying its uplifted remains in the coast ranges of northern California. He has shown that this subduction zone swallowed up entire sea mounts—underseas volcanoes—and then cast them up into the emerging coast range mountains.

Volcanic Violence

Teams of Smithsonian researchers specialize in the study of volcanoes, the often destructive semaphores of crustal movements. The Institution's specialists have been asked by nations in volcanically active regions around the world to assist in times of crisis, and the Institution is recognized internationally as a center for volcanological information.

At the Colombian volcano of Nevada del Ruiz, Melson collected more than 200 samples of rock and pumice. He is examining the specimens for clues to the events and processes that triggered the catastrophic 1985 eruption, which killed 22,000 people. Smithsonian ornithologist Gary Graves surveyed the blast's impact on bird populations. Having documented the volcano's devastating toll—he estimates that up to 95 percent of high-elevation birds were killed—Graves will monitor the recovery process, hoping to learn how catastrophic disturbances influence the evolution and distribution of wildlife in the tropical Andean region. Meanwhile, Vicki Funk, a Smithsonian botanist who specializes in research on the evolution of high-elevation plants, is conducting a long-

term investigation of the eruption's impact on the plants on the upper slopes of the 17,500-foot-high volcano and how they recolonize after the ash flows.

One goal of the Global Volcanism Program in the Department of Mineral Sciences is to gather data on all of the world's active volcanoes and to describe, where possible, their past eruptions. This information will enhance understanding of the processes that lead to volcanic activity, thus improving the possibility of future eruption predictions.

A part of this program is the Global Volcanism Network, formerly known as the Scientific Event Alert Network, which keeps tabs on volcanic activity, as well as on major earthquakes and meteors. With the aid of a global network of about 1,000 observers, GVN workers record vital statistics on these

Museum of Natural History geologist Richard Fiske descends into a fissure on Kilauea Volcano to take measurements of the rate of motion of a gigantic landslide on the volcano's south flank.

Field investigations of shifting sands in southwest Egypt are necessary to verify changes seen in satellite remote sensing data. This campsite borders an area of rapid sand movement, which researchers at the Air and Space Museum and the University of Arizona have been monitoring for more than eight years. (Photo by Ted Maxwell)

events, summing up each month's activity in a newsletter distributed worldwide. More rapid volcano alerts go to satellite specialists, who can then measure the height, dispersal and chemical content of clouds of material disgorged by an eruption.

A central element of the Global Volcanism Program is the Volcano Reference File, a data base of the world's volcanoes and their eruptions during the past 10,000 years. The computerized data base provides current and historical perspectives on activities at the globe's hot spots. This combination of information, explains Tom Simkin, the program's chief scientist, "gives context to today's events and aids identification of past events that may help illuminate tomorrow's."

Two other components of the Global Volcanism Program supplement the growing reference file, providing the raw materials scientists need to explain how volcanoes work. One is the Mineral Sciences Department's collection of specimens from active volcanoes. Totaling about 6,400, the samples are analyzed to understand the genesis of volcanic events. The second component is a volcano archives—a collection of maps, reports, pictures and other documents that describes past eruptions.

The roots of the Smithsonian's long tradition of research on volcanoes date back to 1912, when Charles G. Abbot, then head of the Smithsonian Astrophysical Observatory, studied the atmospheric effects of a major eruption near Katmai in Alaska. While Abbot's study was considered a pioneering effort at the time, such studies are now an integral part of the multidisciplinary field of volcanology. Scientists fully recognize the weather-altering effects of major eruptions.

The development of a coherent picture of global volcanism will require detailed knowledge of the processes afoot at oceanic ridges, where volcanic activity normally goes undetected; at subduction zones, the sites of tectonic collisions where a dense underlying plate plunges into the mantle and potentially violent volcanoes sprout on the lighter, overlying plate; and at "hot spots," areas of volcanic activity that may be far removed from plate boundaries.

Still in preliminary sketches, the picture that finally emerges will be more akin to a collage than a portrait, because volcanism is the product of a confusing array of forces and interactions. Simkin has found, for example, that volcanoes in some regions are much more active and their eruptions much more forceful than volcanoes in geologically similar areas. Melson's analyses have revealed a striking and puzzling variety in the chemical composition of volcanic glasses collected at different oceanic ridges.

The biggest anticipated payoff from studies by Smithsonian researchers and their counterparts around the world would be more accurate prediction of eruptions, especially the densely populated nations clustered near the Pacific Ocean's "ring of fire," including the United States, which ranks third (behind Indonesia and Japan) in the number of historically active volcanoes.

The Geology of Africa

Nearly every year, researchers in the Air and Space Museum's Center for Earth and Planetary Studies vacate their offices and head for sandy, sun-drenched environs. Their destination is not the beach. Rather, it is one of the world's most inhospitable areas: Africa's Sahara Desert and the drought-prone Sahel region to the south. There, CEPS researchers gather "ground-truth" data, on-site

Daniel Stanley, Museum of Natural History geological oceanographer who leads a multinational environmental study of the Nile Delta, takes a break from reviewing data in his field tent east of the Suez Canal.

observations used to check and to interpret the satellite images and remote-sensing measurements that are their main sources of information on the area's terrain and geology.

In the terrestrial portion of the CEPS research program, scientists concentrate on the arid regions of Africa, studying such topics as the movements of sand dunes and human- and climate-induced desertification, the erosive process that transforms arable fringe regions into desert. In one long-term study, CEPS geologist Patricia A. Jacobberger has used satellite-gathered data and her field investigations to trace the effects of a two-decade-long drought on the Inland Niger Delta, a once-verdant region of the Sahel. Comparing aerial photographs taken during the 1950s with satellite data from the 1970s and 1980s, Jacobberger determined that about three-fourths of the delta's "permanent" bodies of water dried up during the drought.

Jacobberger questions whether the region will recover when and if the current siege of arid conditions ends. The Sahel has a long history of alternating periods of drought and adequate rainfall. In years past, the Niger River literally infused the delta with water, branching into channels and subchannels that distributed water throughout the area and deposited fertile sediment on neighboring farmland. But the longevity of the current drought may have wrought irreversible changes that spell the end for rejuvenating the distribution system. A potential outcome, Jacobberger's data suggest, is that the Niger River will be confined to a single master channel, instead of branching like a nerve network through the region. A single river channel might not be able to accommodate even moderate amounts of rainfall, and the result would be destructive floods and increased erosion.

Research by CEPS geologist Ted A. Maxwell has prompted scientists to rethink models of the desertification process. According to the traditional view, migrating sand dunes account for most of the Sahara's expansion. But Maxwell and C. Vance Hayes, a former senior postdoctoral fellow at CEPS, determined that thin, chevron-shaped sheets of sand are, by far, the desert's most active transporters of sand.

Barely discernible at ground level, the chevrons were detected in digitally enhanced images received from remote-sensing satellites. On the basis of field measurements in the hyperarid region of the Sudan, Maxwell and a team of geologists determined that chevrons travel downwind at a rate of up to 500 yards per year, as compared with 10 yards for a typical sand dune. A single chevron only 4 inches thick but three miles wide and half a mile long transports more than half a million cubic yards of sand in a year.

North of the Sudan, in the northeastern part of Egypt's Nile Delta, Daniel J. Stanley, Natural History Museum senior oceanographer, is investigating another type of geological transformation, one with potentially disastrous consequences for the area's 55 million inhabitants. Leader of an international group of scientists participating in the museum's interdisciplinary Mediterranean Basin Project, Stanley has chronicled the delta's subsidence over the past 10,000 years.

Stanley's analyses of drilling cores, some containing samples from about 200 feet below the surface, indicate that parts of the delta have been sinking at a conservatively estimated annual rate of about one-fifth of an inch. Over the last 7,500 years, the northeastern delta dropped at least 125 feet, due mostly, Stanley believes, to movements of faults underlying the area. He proposes that fault movements are literally pulling the northeastern delta apart, causing it to drop like a book shelf when its supports are removed.

Beyond showing that the area is not on "solid ground," Stanley's geological scenario depicts the complex interactions between natural processes and human actions. During the region's recent geological past, land subsidence has been countered by another natural process, the deposition of sediments by the migrating channels of the Nile. As the region's substrate sank, the influx of sediments has offset vertical displacement. With construction of the Aswan Dam in the mid-1960s, however, the balance was destroyed. Reduced supplies of sediment may not be able to counter the lowering. Meanwhile, erosion along Egypt's Mediterranean coast has accelerated, also as a result of decreased input of sediment.

These developments set the stage for disaster. By the year 2100, according to some projections, the world sea level may rise by more than 1½ feet; over the same period, Stanley estimates, the northeastern delta will subside by a like amount. As a result, much of the region within about 20 miles of the coast, which includes the city of Port Said and the area bordering the northern part of the Suez Canal, would be under water. With this loss of land of about 15 percent, salt in the ground water will increase in the Nile Delta, reducing further already diminished agricultural production. Given the dire implications of this prediction for the rapidly growing population, Stanley is pursuing more detailed studies of the northeastern delta's subsidence.

Coastal dunes encroaching on agricultural lands and former lagoons in Egypt's Nile Delta are posing food-supply threats to the region. (Photo by Daniel Stanley)

Studies conducted by the Tropical Research Institute on Barro Colorado Island, which include documenting its richness of plants, have been instrumental in improving our knowledge of biological processes in the tropics. (Photo by Carl Hansen)

Life on Earth

Life is at once mundane and remarkable. It is mundane because the starting materials are so common. The raw elements that make up lowly dirt are identical to those assembled to create the planet's most highly evolved organism, *Homo sapiens*. Ponder the packaging steps in between — evolution — and one must acknowledge the incredible.

Evolution, the framework upon which all of biology rests, is understood in only the broadest of terms. The Earth's current inventory of plant and animal species — estimated to number between 5 million and 30 million — followed curious evolutionary paths, and the relationships among species are often obscured.

Consider the plight of the dinosaurs, the planet's dominant organisms for about 150 million years. Mammals were also present during this period, but they were confined to a lesser niche. The largest were probably no bigger than a raccoon. Then, 65 million years ago, the reign of the dinosaurs ended in a massive extinction event. A new pecking order developed, one that favored mammalian species and, eventually, the emergence of modern humans. But the evolutionary line of the dinosaurs was not completely severed; rather, it gave rise to modern crocodiles and birds.

Variations on that sequence of evolutionary progression characterize all of life. The most amazing thing that can be said about these seemingly strange events is that there is "rhyme and reason" to all of it. Through their studies, Smithsonian scientists are deciphering the complex logic and cadence of evolution.

Much of this research comprises studies of the origin, history and interrelationships of living systems. By necessity, Smithsonian scientists must study details — features of anatomy and behavior, as well as sequences of genes — that may eventually reveal how one species is related to another, why a particular group of organisms has survived while a similar population has perished and how changes in environment have helped steer the course of evolution. They must study all of Earth, because clues to the evolutionary past and future are scattered about the surface of the planet and in the fossils buried below. To construct the natural histories of groups of organisms, Smithsonian scientists must analyze numerous specimens to distinguish real evolutionary change from accidental variation.

Clarifying Species Relationships

Biologists at the Natural History Museum trace the lines of descent that link one group of organisms to another. The basis for their studies is sys-

The incredible diversity of life is reflected in the face of a royal fly-catcher, captured on the banks of the Rio Xingu in eastern Brazil. The red crest, unique to this one of 300 species of flycatchers, continues to intrigue ornithologists. A Smithsonian study was launched to assist Brazil in surveying the biological diversity of the region. (Photo by Gary Graves)

Amuseum or a zoo may seem an unlikely place to find molecular biologists who work at the leading edge of science. But, in fact, behind the scenes at the Smithsonian, scientists are putting to work the research tools of biotechnology—an array of techniques to examine and manipulate genetic material—to answer questions about evolution and help conserve some of the world's endangered species.

"This technology has affected every field of biology," says Dr. Michael Braun, program director of the Laboratory of Molecular Systematics operated by the Natural History Museum. "Evolutionary biologists are now jumping on the bandwagon in force."

Braun's laboratory is one of the premiere facilities in the nation for this kind of work, which includes studies of DNA, the basic molecule of all life. It has counterparts at the National Zoological Park and the Smithsonian Tropical Research Institute.

The research can help determine whether two different animals descended from the same ancestor. Other work includes determining the relationships among several families of animals and understanding better the mechanisms of evolution.

The labs will also deliver data for research on population genetics—the diversity in a species' gene pool. Zoos find this information valuable as they seek to design breeding programs for endangered species.

The Molecular Systematics Lab at the Smithsonian's Museum Support Center in Suitland, Md., is a high-tech world. There, the gleaming glassware and scientific instruments include ultracentrifuge machines for separating types of DNA; autoclaves for sterilizing instruments; ultra-cold freezers for storing such specimens as plant and animal tissue; and automated DNA synthesis equipment.

Many of the studies, Braun says, involve tracing the evolutionary development of organisms. He cites the analy-

Patricia Sawaya and Tom Parsons, research fellows at the Museum of Natural History's Laboratory of Molecular Systematics, examine DNA patterns that show genetic differences among chickadees. (Photo by Doc Dougherty)

sis of genetic material from humans, gorillas and chimpanzees. Molecular evolutionists, he says, have shown that humans and chimps appear to be more closely related to each other than chimps and gorillas, despite physical appearances that suggest otherwise.

For traditional systematics, researchers trace evolutionary development by examining "morphologic traits"—physical characteristics. These traits are compared with those of other living animals or plants or with specimens from the fossil record. Scientists who study systematics slowly build a body of data about an organism's evolution and its relationship to other organisms. Still, the fossil record is often incomplete, and morphological traits are only one reflection of the organism. Conclusions drawn by one scientist may be contradicted by a colleague.

Enter molecular biology. Since the genome of any organism contains vast amounts of information, Braun says, researchers at the Molecular Systematics

Lab can provide data to fill in the blanks or resolve disputes arising from different interpretations. Still, "we can't ignore the fossil evidence," Braun says. "It provides the framework for the interpretation of the molecular data." Most of this data involves techniques that directly or indirectly examine an organism's DNA.

One technique is electrophoresis, which involves extracting proteins from an animal's blood or tissue and testing the samples. Because DNA determines the type of proteins in an organism, researchers can infer the relatedness of similar organisms through statistical analysis of the proteins.

Other molecular techniques include "DNA fingerprinting." The DNA of each plant or animal, like a human fingerprint, is unique. "Polymerase chain reaction," another of the field's latest developments, allows scientists to look at subtypes of DNA previously beyond their grasp. In fact, "any molecular genetic technique developed is one we might be able to use," Braun says. ✳

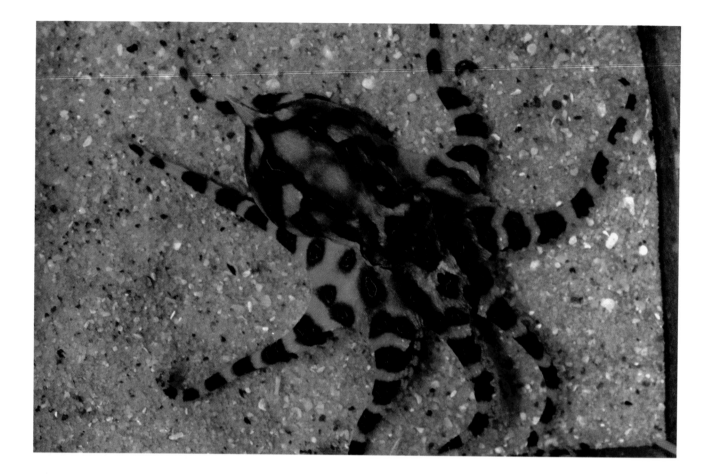

Museum of Natural History scientist Clyde Roper found that the deadly poisonous blue-ringed octopus, previously thought to be only two species, was actually a whole complex of closely related species. Working with live animals, Roper and a colleague discovered color, pattern and texture, not visible on study specimens, that facilitated a new approach to octopod and cuttlefish systematics. (Photo by Clyde Roper)

tematics and taxonomy. These terms are not strictly synonymous. Systematics deals with discovering phylogenetic, or "family tree," relationships through study of patterns of character variation. Taxonomy deals with sorting organisms into categories and then assigning names to those categories. A phylogenetic tree shows how the forces of natural selection have shaped plants and animals. For organisms that genetically adapt to new environmental conditions, the reward is survival. Organisms that fail to adapt face extinction.

Many of the Institution's taxonomists are the acknowledged world experts in their animal and plant specialties. Collectively, their investigations and the resulting descriptions of plant and animal life help reveal the evolution of the natural world. Many blanks in this picture remain to be filled. Yet the work done so far clearly shows that each living species plays a role in the global ecosystem. That fact alone explains the need for comprehensive systematics research. But there are other reasons as well.

Consider the taxonomic specialty of invertebrate zoologist Clyde F. E. Roper: cephalopods, a class of mollusks that includes the octopus, the squid and the cuttlefish. To clean up some of the confusion surrounding these poorly understood animals,

Roper convened an international workshop focusing on seven critical families of cephalopods. The researchers who gathered at the Smithsonian evaluated thousands of specimens and clarified evolutionary relationships among species. The intensive effort pinned down key anatomical features that aid classification and helped the scientists assemble important information about the animals' geographic distribution, diet, predators and competitors.

Given the interrelationships inherent in nature, this understanding leads to other benefits. As information on cephalopods grows, knowledge of tunas, dolphins, sharks, toothed whales, seals and other cephalopod predators also increases.

Moreover, growing demand for squid and octopus, a major part of the human diet in Asia and other areas of the world, introduces the danger of overharvesting. "If we overfish cephalopods," Roper explains, "we could have an adverse impact on populations of fishes, marine mammals and birds. It's the old question: How much can we take today and still be sure that there will be enough next year and the next?"

Knowledge gained from the studies conducted by Roper and his colleagues can guide the development of sound fisheries-management practices. It may also reveal aquaculture methods for raising cephalopods, which might ease pressure from overfishing. Finally, better understanding of the relationships between cephalopod species benefits research efforts in medicine. The squid's giant nerve cell, for example, is an enlarged model for study of human nerve tissue. In addition, novel chemical compounds found in cephalopods could lead to the development of new anti-shock, anesthetic and anti-parasite drugs.

Evolutionary Processes

Phylogenetic trees serve as road maps, tracing the evolutionary routes that led living species to their current forms and ecological niches. The journeys from past to present are more like meanderings than direct, non-stop trips.

In the ponds and rivers of Brazil are tiny fishes, including some familiar to aquarium hobbyists. A typical aquarium tank, however, would not hold their much larger ancestors. Stanley H. Weitzman, a researcher in the Department of Vertebrate Zoology at the Museum of Natural History, is studying the evolution-directed process of miniaturization. Part of his research entails comparing the costs and benefits of a species' change from a large to a small body. In contrast, his department colleague, G. David Johnson, also studies tiny fishes, but from a different perspective. Focusing frequently on fishes that live along the shores of the Pacific and Indian oceans, Johnson searches for clues to their evolutionary relationships in the form and structure of their planktonic larval stages, many of which look strikingly different from the adults.

An important issue among biologists is whether evolution occurs as a series of gradual changes, as Darwin maintained, or whether the past is punctuated by abrupt bursts of evolutionary change. Alan Cheetham's studies of bryozoan fossils, the ancestors of the tiny aquatic animals that encrust submerged surfaces or form fan-shaped colonies, lend support to the so-called punctuated-equilibrium model where long periods of little change are interrupted by brief periods of rapid change.

An invertebrate paleobiologist at the Natural History Museum, Cheetham examined fossils of nine bryozoan species that lived in the Caribbean region during a 4.5-million-year span that includes parts of the Pliocene and Miocene epochs during which many modern plants and animals developed. Unlike past studies of this type, which have focused on changes in single body characteristics, Cheetham's investigation analyzed numerous traits simultaneously to assess the degree of change in the overall structure and form of the organisms.

Using advanced computer techniques and statistical methods, the paleobiologist found that, within each bryozoan species, morphological changes were too slow and too discontinuous to give rise to new species. Most change was concentrated into brief periods, geologically speaking, during which new species arose. Cheetham's exhaustive study suggests that the motor that drives evolutionary change is not permanently set on cruise-control, but is subject to episodes of acceleration and deceleration. Some past events induced rapid change and the emergence of new species. These episodes, however, appear to have been followed by long periods of little or no change. Hence the name, "punctuated equilibrium."

For Jonathan Coddington, an arachnologist at the museum, the web-weaving patterns of spiders serve as a window on the complexities of evolutionary change. His studies challenge interpreta-

Museum of Natural History arachnologist Jonathan Coddington collects specimens in Peru as part of his continuing study of spiders and their web-weaving practices. (Photo by Chip Clark)

The islands of the world are home to thousands of species of birds, most of them uniquely adapted to the special attributes of insular ecosystems. Unfortunately, these ecosystems are vulnerable to disruptive forces.

Recent events on Guam in the western Pacific demonstrate just how fragile these ecosystems can be. There, brown tree snakes that stole in aboard military transport ships during World War II have devastated populations of forest birds. The introduced predator eliminated all but two native species and was well on the way to finishing the job when researchers from the National Zoo and other organizations embarked on a major captive-breeding and species-reintroduction effort.

As of 1984, the number of Guam rails had fallen to 18 and Guam kingfishers to 32. Since then, captive-breeding programs at the National Zoo and other zoos have increased the rail population to more than 100 and the kingfishers to about 50. Still ahead is the formidable task of establishing viable populations in the wild.

But research by scientists at the Smithsonian's Museum of Natural History and their colleagues indicates that the pattern of human-caused extinctions seen on Guam, rather than being a modern phenomenon, is one that began in prehistoric times. In the Hawaiian Islands, Storrs Olson and Helen James, along with others, have uncovered fossils of about 50 species of birds that became extinct during prehistoric times, approximately doubling the number previously known. Radiocarbon analyses trace the prehistoric extinctions to after the year 400, coinciding with the arrival of the Polynesian peoples who first colonized the island chain.

The cause of these extinctions is thought to be primarily the destruction of lowland forests by human agriculturalists, abetted by hunting and the depredations of introduced predators, herbivores and possibly even pathogens. The extinctions documented for Hawaii are hardly isolated phenomena. Investigations of fossils from New Zealand, Madagascar and many other oceanic islands are revealing a similar pattern of prehistoric, human-caused extinctions. The islands affected are spread over the Pacific, Atlantic and Indian oceans, as well as the Caribbean and Mediterranean seas. These findings suggest that biologists, who have largely concerned themselves with surviving island wildlife, lack a comprehensive picture of the species composition and biological diversity of island environments. Assembling such a picture is a major goal of the Evolution of Island Ecosystems project at the Museum of Natural History.

The project's findings could have far-reaching implications. Olson and James have speculated that, for the Hawaiian Islands, the number of unknown species wiped out by human activities could exceed the documented total of historically known species. As a result, theories of evolution, ecology and conservation that draw heavily from studies of island wildlife may have to be re-examined. ✹

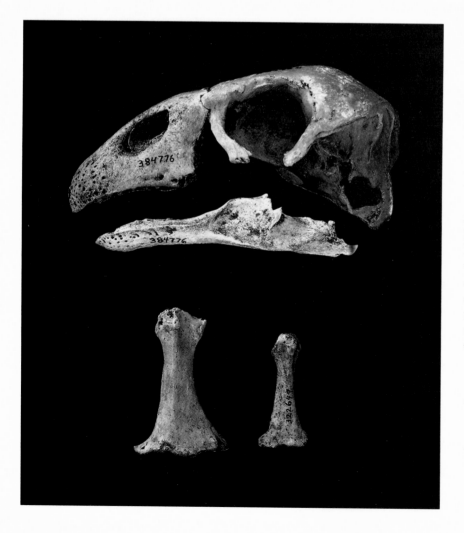

These bones, thought to be less than 10,000 years old, are from the "moa-nalos," meaning lost fowl, one of about 56 species that have become extinct in Hawaii in the last 2,000 years. The search for fossil bones on islands around the world by Museum of Natural History scientists is revealing that widespread animal extinctions were associated with human migration throughout Oceania.

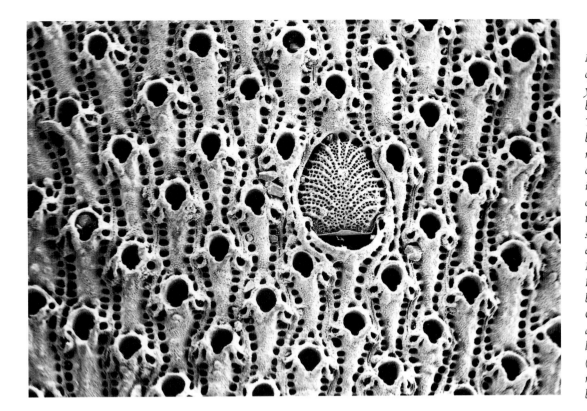

Microscopic detail of a 2-million-year-old fossil of a bryozoan colony. The distance between the larger, more-or-less circular openings is about 4/100ths of an inch. These tiny details of structure are one element studied by Museum of Natural History paleobiologist Alan Cheetham to distinguish biological species. (Scanning electron microscope image by Mary Mann)

tions of one of Darwin's primary tenets: adaptation through natural selection. The core of the theory of evolution, this tenet predicts that those genetic changes that confer advantages will prevail, thereby improving the match between surviving species and their environments.

Coddington's research does not contradict this principle, but it does question scientific explanations for some seemingly successful adaptations. Too often, Coddington maintains, the explanations are based on perceptions of current situations rather than on dispassionate reconstruction of evolutionary history.

A case in point is the origin of orb webs, a topic that has fueled debate for nearly a century. In many ways geometric masterpieces, the circular snares are nearly as regular in their construction as the molecular latticework of a crystal. Most scientists have viewed the web architecture as the crowning achievement of spider evolution. By comparison, according to the standard interpretation, irregular cobwebs—the kind that you might find in out-of-the-way corners of your home—are a primitive architectural mess, at least to the human eye.

To account for the fact that two very distantly related groups of spiders, which were supposed to have split from the evolutionary tree before the first orb web was spun, now make very sim-

ilar circular snares, scientists invoked the concept of "convergent evolution." With the aid of the forces of natural selection, the two groups independently arrived at the same elegant solution—the orb web—to capturing prey.

Long hours of observing the web forms and weaving behaviors of members of both spider groups has led Coddington to an entirely different, and simpler, conclusion. As they build their hubs, spin their frame lines and radii, and carry out the other steps involved in erecting an orb web, both types of spiders follow essentially the same routine. The orb design, however, is not so restrictive as to dictate a single web-building procedure.

The aesthetic appeal of the orb web notwithstanding, Coddington has deduced that the apparently sophisticated construction is really a primitive inherited trait and not a highly derived adapted trait that had two evolutionary origins. The two groups, which together comprise one-third of all spiders, descended from an ancestor that built webs of similar circular design.

"Far from confirming that the orb web is the adaptive pinnacle of spider-web architecture . . . ," Coddington has written, "the evidence suggests that the orb web is an ancient feature, discarded by many derived" groups of spiders. Counter to intuition, the orb did not "emerge from the chaos of the cobweb," he added. "It was the other way around."

The Evolution of Ecosystems

Rather than concentrating on individual groups of organisms, new interdisciplinary teams of Smithsonian biologists, paleontologists and anthropologists are evaluating the Earth's evolutionary history from the perspective of plant and animal communities and their habitats as integrated wholes. This novel and exciting approach extends the science of ecology—the study of the relationships between present-day organisms and their environments—to the fossil record.

"Nothing evolves by itself," paleobiologist Anna K. Behrensmeyer explains. Her specialty is "taphonomy," the study of how information recorded in the fossil record is affected by the processes that preserved it, and she is one of four paleobiologists directing the Natural History Museum's program on the Evolution of Terrestrial Ecosystems. Like its two counterpart programs, which address marine and island ecosystems (see "Island Ecosystems," Page 44), this program seeks to determine how environmental changes influenced the course of evolution. In turn, information on the biological responses of plants and animals to past episodes of ecosystem disruption and instability will help scientists understand the implications of current environmental problems.

Indeed, there are striking parallels between past and present. About 100 million years ago, for example, the Earth underwent a warming trend, either the cause or the result of a buildup of carbon dioxide in the atmosphere. Today, we worry about the climatic warming predicted to be the consequence of growing atmospheric concentrations of carbon dioxide and other "greenhouse"

gases, many of them the byproducts of fossil-fuel burning and other human activities.

Over the 400-million-year span the program encompasses, plants and animals have changed radically. Yet certain themes and roles are repeated throughout, as revealed by the fossil record. Again, the most celebrated of extinction events serves as an example. When the dinosaurs died off, mammals were, in effect, waiting in the wings to carry out the ecological roles vacated by the mass extinction. Environmental influences that eliminated the dinosaurs, it appears, ultimately gave mammals the chance to fill the empty niches.

Though their biology is markedly different from that of dinosaurs, mammals seem to have been "preadapted" to their elevated ecological status. All they needed was a chance, the opportunity afforded by the demise of dinosaurs. This example—and there are many to draw from—suggests that ecosystems impose general constraints on evolution. Within this ecological framework, the forces of natural selection act to shape the specialization of individual species.

Smithsonian scientists are building a data base that will help them and collaborators from around the world discern the chain of ecological cause and effect since the Silurian period some 425 million years ago. Rather than listing family relationships, the data base groups organisms according to important attributes, including size, shape, feeding mechanisms, feeding behaviors and habitats.

With this information available on computer, scientists can compare the species that inhabited a particular kind of ecosystem over geological time and determine what ecological factors influenced the makeup of plant and animal communities. If a species—*Homo sapiens,* for example—expanded its range, researchers might be able to identify adaptations that helped it adjust to new surroundings.

The three programs on the evolution of ecosystems complement each other and reaffirm the Smithsonian's long-established commitment to evolution and ecology, which is part and parcel of systematics research. "We don't study species because we're stamp collectors," invertebrate zoologist Klaus Ruetzler explains. "I do systematics because it's a fundamental tool in ecology." And, particularly in today's world, systematics and ecology are essential to conservation.

Ruetzler directs the Smithsonian's Caribbean Coral Reef Ecosystems program, an interdisciplinary study of the geology, biology, physical dynamics, and natural history of Caribbean reefs and mangroves near Carrie Bow Cay off the coast of

Mireya Correa (right), a botanist with the Tropical Research Institute and the University of Panama, has found that the "rare" garbage plant, whose leaves trap forest understory debris, occurs commonly in the cloud forest of Panama's Campana National Park. (Photo by Carl Hansen)

When a California museum several years ago hired a curator of marine mammals, the Smithsonian's James Mead lost his claim to uniqueness. At Mead's urging, the Los Angeles County Museum of Natural History had created the new position, deposing him as America's sole curator of marine mammals.

As far as Mead is concerned, the field could use more practitioners because so little is known about whales, dolphins and other marine mammals. Yet the National Museum of Natural History, where Mead works in the Department of Vertebrate Zoology, is one of the few places in the world committed to collecting and studying these animals. "Frankly, these large animals are a pain to most museum administrators because they take up so much storage space," Mead says. "Early on, this Institution demonstrated a commitment to performing classic taxonomic studies of marine mammals and has stuck with it."

Thus, Mead and other successors to Spencer Fullerton Baird, the Smithsonian secretary who began collecting marine mammals in the late 1800s, have added much to scientific understanding of marine mammals. In contrast, many museums jettisoned their collections, some of which have been inherited by the Smithsonian. Others kept their initial holdings but moved them to off-site repositories where the specimens are rarely studied.

Like so many of the collections cared for by the Museum of Natural History, the marine mammal collection is the largest in the world, but still not large enough for studies needed to fill important gaps in understanding marine mammals.

In 1972, Congress directed the museum to create the Marine Mammal Program to monitor the mid-Atlantic coast for strandings of marine mammals. The program was a product of the Marine Mammal Protection Act, which forbids commercial exploitation

Working with Museum of Natural History curator James Mead, Charley Potter (left) and William McLellan of the collections management team begin the investigation into the cause of death of a 52-foot-long male sperm whale that washed ashore dead in January 1987 near Cape Hatteras, N.C. (Photo by Chip Clark)

of a variety of marine mammals in U.S. coastal waters and prohibits scientists from collecting live animals for research purposes.

Since then, Mead and his assistants have been collecting and studying carcasses of marine mammals stranded on coastal beaches. Through their educational efforts, the Smithsonian team has created a voluntary surveillance network of wildlife officials, marina operators and others who contact the Marine Mammal Program when they discover a stranded animal.

Because of this vigilance, Mead was quick to sound an alarm in 1987 when an unprecedented number of bottlenose dolphins started washing ashore.

Hundreds of dolphins died that summer, triggering an investigation by an international team of researchers that included Mead and other Smithsonian scientists. A naturally occurring toxin was eventually found to be the cause of the deaths.

Although the major die-off was a tragedy, the more than 300 dolphin specimens added to the Smithsonian's collection will support research that may eventually yield knowledge valuable for protecting dolphin populations. "We're finding out how little we know about these animals because of the deaths," Mead says. "There's lots of general knowledge about dolphins, but little of the data that science demands." ✳

Belize. The long-term investigation of this barrier reef system, second in size only to Australia's Great Barrier Reef, involves 70 scientists from 30 institutions around the world. Summarized in a thick monograph, the combined effort yielded the most comprehensive assay available of life and its underpinnings in a reef ecosystem. The findings greatly enhance understanding of all reef communities, the most biologically productive ecosystems in the world, and the Smithsonian expects such studies to be useful in efforts to safeguard these imperiled marine habitats.

To the Ends of the Earth and Places in Between

To enhance understanding of life on Earth—the encompassing mission of the Smithsonian's biological studies—the Institution's scientists must respond to research opportunities wherever they exist. Volcanologists journey to the sites of new eruptions; botanists comb Andean cloud forests to find and study new plants; geologists and invertebrate zoologists descend into or even reach the ocean bottom to study sea-floor spreading and the bizarre life forms that grow near the seething vents;

and mammalogists trek to the sites of strandings of dolphins, whales and other marine mammals (see "Mysteries of Marine Mammals," Page 47).

The examples are many, but each typifies the Smithsonian's commitment to uncovering new sections to the mystery story of life on Earth. Indeed, the Institution's quest has contributed key clues to unraveling the mystery. But discoveries inevitably have a humbling effect. The more we learn, the more we recognize the limits of current human understanding. To leave a stone unturned in the pursuit of biological knowledge is to leave blank a page in the Earth's story.

Plumbing the Depths of the Ocean

Nearly a decade after the first Apollo astronauts landed on the moon, marine researchers began journeying to previously inaccessible destinations that, in some ways, held more surprises than the lunar surface. Submersible research vessels, as cramped as the command modules that held the Apollo astronauts, are transporting scientists to the abyssal depths, down to the oceanic vents that spew hot, sulfur-laden waters into the sea. In this

stygian environment, Smithsonian researchers and their counterparts from other institutions have found an unexpectedly rich variety of life.

Much of the job of describing the members of these odd communities has been assigned to Smithsonian biologists. Perhaps the most striking are the giant plume worms—some are 11 feet long and 4 inches around—that thrive in an ecosystem devoid of plants, the essential building blocks, or so it was thought, of all food chains. Meredith Jones, who recently retired as an invertebrate zoologist at the Museum of Natural History, played a key role in explaining this important exception.

Jones and his colleagues determined that the worms, which lack a mouth and gut, are sustained by sulfur-consuming bacteria that flourish in this dark realm. The bacteria, absorbed through the bright red tentacles that sprout like feathers from the worms' tips, line the animals' body cavities. Carbohydrates manufactured by the bacteria are harvested by the worms through mechanisms now under study. But an exception to the food-chain rule is now established; sunlight and photosynthesis are not prerequisites for life.

Continuing exploration of the oceanic depths will certainly reveal more surprises and challenges to scientists. And many of these developments likely will begin with the descriptive and interpretive biological studies of Smithsonian scientists.

Consider the chain of events that began with the recovery of a heretofore unidentified shrimp collected by the National Marine Fisheries Service, one of several federal agencies that assign scientists to residence at the museum and deposit specimens in its research collection. Austin Williams, an invertebrate zoologist with NMFS, assigned to the museum, conducted the initial taxonomic investigation of the 3-inch-long eyeless shrimp, collected during an expedition to the mid-Atlantic Ridge.

Building on the results of the investigation, Williams' collaborator, Cindy Lee Van Dover, a graduate student at the Woods Hole Oceanographic Institution in Massachusetts, conducted a detailed study of the eyeless shrimp's physiology. Over the course of several months, she discovered that beneath the animal's translucent shell was an array of primitive light receptors containing the light-sensitive pigment rhodopsin. (The retina of the human eye contains the same chemical.) But why would an animal that lives in absolute darkness have biological equipment for perceiving light?

That question still awaits a definitive answer, but another recent finding has yielded a tantaliz-

ing clue. During a scientific expedition along the Juan de Fuca Ridge off Canada's west coast, an extremely sensitive camera detected a faint glow some 7,200 feet below the surface. Like a candle's flame, the light—too dim to be seen with the unaided eye—emanated from the top of one of the pillarlike structures that form near the ridge.

What generates the light and whether the shrimp can perceive the dim glow are among the many questions that follow from this discovery. An intriguing possibility is that the light may be sufficient to generate photosynthetic reactions in submarine realms far beyond the reach of sunlight. If so, speculation that life on the ocean bottom began early in the Earth's history would benefit from this new piece of evidence.

But how much light is needed for photosynthesis, the process by which plants use light energy to convert water and carbon dioxide into food? The answer, botanists from the Natural History Museum and a colleague from the Harbor Branch Oceanographic Institution Inc. discovered, is a lot less than scientists had believed.

Surveying the underwater plants near San Salvador Island, about 380 miles southeast of Miami, the research team, headed by Smithsonian botanists Mark and Diane Littler, discovered an uncharted sea mount, its slopes rich with plant life.

Beginning at a depth of about 1,700 feet, the team's tiny but versatile submersible craft ascended slowly. Nearly halfway from the surface, the scene before the researchers changed remarkably. Almost 900 feet down, a depth impenetrable to all but about 0.0009 percent of the light striking the ocean surface, a purple coralline alga was growing the way all plants do, by means of photosynthesis.

The discovery by the Littlers' team smashed the record for the deepest known plant life. More important, it required revision of a prevailing concept. Until the purple, crust-forming alga was found, most scientists postulated that plants could not live below a depth of about 650 feet, known as the "compensation level." At this depth, the scientists had maintained, a plant would consume more energy than it could produce photosynthetically. But the plant discovered by the Smithsonian team thrived at the 900-foot level, forming extensive blankets of crust. With a photosynthetic efficiency about 100 times greater than that of plants just below the surface, the newly discovered species of algae makes the most of its scant allotment of solar energy.

Beyond attesting to the ability of marine plants to adapt to virtual darkness, the new alga must be considered in broader contexts, as a constituent of the marine food web, as a builder of reefs in tropical waters and as a contributor to many other processes that sustain life in the oceans.

Nature's Isolated Outposts

The world is crowded, but there are still sites where the dynamic forces of nature have proceeded with little or no human intervention. Many of these sites are islands, especially good areas for studying the processes of evolution. One such island—Barro Colorado Island in Panama—is in the custodianship of the Smithsonian. Through its participation in several international foundations, the Institution helps preserve for research other ecologically important enclaves, including Ecuador's Galapagos Islands, the site of Darwin's pioneering studies of evolution.

The Aldabra atoll—a coral-capped submarine volcano more than 200 miles east of Africa in the Indian Ocean—typifies the scientific value of preserving and studying these isolated outposts. Darwin was one of the first scientists to recognize the uniqueness of Aldabra in the 1860s. More than a century later, Aldabra was designated a World Heritage site, thanks, in part, to the Smithsonian's efforts.

From above, Aldabra resembles a misshapen wedding ring. A narrow margin of land surrounds a shallow lagoon. Aldabra barely pokes out above the ocean, and at various times in past eons, the atoll has been submerged. Each episode marked the end of one ecosystem and the beginning of another, a pattern revealed by the fossils embedded in Aldabra's limestone layers.

A trip to Aldabra today is a trip back in time, to the Cretaceous period some 100 million years ago when reptiles were the Earth's dominant organisms. The atoll's dominant species is the Indian Ocean's giant tortoise. The 150,000 tortoises that live on the island are survivors; heavy exploitation wiped out giant tortoise populations on islands elsewhere.

Interdisciplinary teams of Smithsonian scientists regularly visit Aldabra to study its terrestrial and marine plants and animals, many of which can be found nowhere else in the world. From these complementary efforts come insights into the workings of the island ecosystem, the interplay of environmental and evolutionary forces that have combined to produce this incomparable collection of life.

Invertebrate zoologist Brian Kensley, the Smithsonian scientist who led the most recent expeditions to Aldabra, has found an amazing diversity of shrimp and other crustaceans in the island's sinkholes, small water-filled caves that dot the surface. Despite their proximity and apparent similarity, the sinkholes are mini-ecosystems; some contain crustacean and fish species not found in other pools. Determining the factors responsible for these communities is one of Kensley's goals.

More enigmatic for Kensley and his colleagues, however, is a striking similarity. Aldabra's sinkholes contain tiny crustaceans identical to those found in similar pools on islands half a world away. Scientists face the quandary of explaining how the organisms traversed such great distances. Could it be, as one theory suggests, that the crustaceans are biological relics from before the breakup of the continents, separated by the movements of the Earth's crustal plates? That is but one of the many fascinating riddles posed by the Aldabra ecosystem.

The Chesapeake Bay

Anyone who has visited the Chesapeake Bay would concur with Capt. John Smith's description of the nation's largest estuary nearly 400 years ago: "Heaven and earth never agreed better to frame a place for man's habitation." But modern history has tinged these words with irony, for the bay's appeal has helped undermine its ecological health.

Accelerating development along the bay's 8,000 miles of shoreline has strained the estuary's resiliency. Pollution, especially excessive loading of nutrients and toxic materials, has severely degraded water quality, resulting in calamitous declines in commercially important fish and shellfish populations.

Since the early 1970s, the Smithsonian Environmental Research Center, located on the Rhode River, a subestuary of the Chesapeake Bay, has been conducting long-term studies of the array of natural and human-caused phenomena that influence the bay's ecology. Sophisticated sampling systems and automated instruments for monitoring ozone and carbon-dioxide levels, water chemistry, soil runoff and other important environmental variables are strategically placed throughout the 2,600-acre watershed that the Center occupies. Analyses of the data provided by this continuous surveillance system are helping SERC scientists unmask key influences—acting alone or in combination—at work in the ecosystem. In turn, the results of these analyses are used to develop models for linking cause and effect in the complex environment. A recent study demonstrates the importance of taking this approach.

Early efforts to curb water pollution were aimed at point sources—storm-sewer pipes and industrial dischargers of effluents. Later studies revealed that such overland runoff as rainwater and snowmelt draining from agricultural fields was also a

David Correll, director of the Environmental Research Center, collects a water sample as part of an ongoing acid rain study being conducted near the Chesapeake Bay in Maryland. (Photo by Dane Penland)

Despite widespread predictions of the "greenhouse effect"—global warming due to increasing amounts of atmospheric carbon dioxide—little is known about the effects of increased carbon dioxide on the world's vegetation. Bert Drake, a plant physiologist at the Smithsonian Environmental Research Center, has designed an innovative experiment that exposes wild salt-marsh plants to twice the amount of today's atmospheric level of carbon dioxide, which globally averages more than 353 parts per million. A doubling of atmospheric carbon dioxide from the pre-industrial level of about 270 to more than 540 parts per million is expected to occur during the next century.

The studies are important, Drake says, because the chief cause of increasing levels of carbon dioxide in the atmosphere—the burning of fossil fuels, particularly in developed nations—shows few signs of abating. Moreover, the response of the world's vegetation to an increase in atmospheric carbon dioxide holds implications for world climates and the carbon cycle, the circulation of carbon—a basic element of all organic compounds—between the atmosphere, the land vegetation and the oceans.

The oceans are the Earth's biggest pool of carbon, followed by the land masses and the atmosphere. Plants act as a "sink" for a large portion of terrestrial carbon by their own uptake and storage of carbon dioxide. Photosynthesis is stimulated by rising levels of atmospheric carbon dioxide. Plants also release carbon dioxide, however, through their own respiration, when they decompose or when they are burned. In predicting future climates, Drake says, researchers need to know how these two competing processes—the uptake and loss of carbon by plants—will influence the atmospheric pool of carbon.

At the Center's 2,600-acre facility on a subestuary of the Chesapeake Bay, Drake and his assistants have constructed an elaborate network of clear polyester chambers that isolate groups of plants on a marsh. The chambers are divided into three groups, with 10 chambers per group.

Carbon dioxide from tanks is released 24 hours a day into half of the chambers in each of the three groups, doubling the daytime ambient amount of this gas to nearly 700 parts per million. An ingenious system of blowers assures that plants within the chambers experience the same environment as those in marsh areas outside the chambers.

In addition to studying the effect of carbon dioxide on plant growth, Drake and his team measure water loss and photosynthesis for individual plants and for all the plants in a given chamber. Plants experience water stress when their supply of water cannot keep pace with the demand of evaporation, and elevated carbon dioxide is expected to reduce water loss and thus to alleviate water stress.

The main findings of the study are that rising atmospheric carbon dioxide concentration increased carbon uptake and storage by the salt marsh ecosystems. While the greenhouse effect will no doubt have major consequences—many of them dire—Drake cautions against a sole focus on these aspects. The world's vegetation might thrive in this atmosphere and, perhaps, fix and store significant amounts of the additional atmospheric carbon dioxide. "The most useful approach is to examine it from all aspects of rising carbon dioxide and climate change," he says, "not just the potentially negative effects." ✳

Open-top chambers expose marsh plants to elevated levels of atmospheric carbon dioxide in studies at the Environmental Research Center. (Photo by Bert Drake)

significant contributor of pollutants. But the dynamics of water pollution are even more complicated than this.

On the basis of an analysis of seven years worth of monitoring data, Center director David L. Correll and visiting researcher Deborah Ford determined that precipitation directly deposits significant amounts of nitrogen into the Rhode River. On average, the annual influx of rain-borne nitrogen is nearly equal to the amount of the nutrient discharged by land runoff. During summer and fall, rain is the primary external source of nitrogen. Moreover, the long-term analysis—the first of its kind—revealed increasing concentrations of nitrogen in precipitation, a trend that corresponds with growing nitrogen-oxide emissions resulting from increasing consumption of fossil fuels. Using similar research approaches, SERC scientists and visiting investigators have evaluated the acidity of rainfall in the watershed and the acidity of drainage waters and groundwater originating in different parts of the ecosystem. They have also studied the effectiveness of coastal vegetation as a buffer against pollution.

Other studies focus on the watershed's terrestrial and aquatic plants and animals. An ongoing investigation of the bay's most celebrated resident, the blue crab, has yielded important new information about the animal's ecology. SERC biologist Anson Hines and his collaborators have used small ultrasonic tags to track crab movements and to learn about various aspects of crab behavior, including when the animals are eating and the size of their prey.

SERC research is directly relevant to efforts to safeguard the bay, but it also addresses environmental issues of global concern. One project intends to decipher the complexities of the Earth's changing atmosphere, monitoring, for example, the intensity of ultraviolet radiation, which reflects sunspot cycles and the ozone content of the stratosphere. Another study evaluates the effects of changing carbon-dioxide concentrations on plant growth and competition (see "Carbon Dioxide and a Salt Marsh," Page 52).

Environmental modeling studies at the Natural History Museum complement the on-site investigations at the Smithsonian's Chesapeake Bay facility. At the museum, Walter Adey, director of the Marine Systems Laboratory, has re-created the bay in a basement laboratory. Adey's large microhabitat simulates ecological conditions in the bay, replicating changing tides and other natural processes at work in the estuarine environment.

The miniature bay—like Adey's living models of the Caribbean coral reef and Maine coastal en-

vironment on exhibit in the museum—is a tool for determining the various processes that govern the ecosystem. Variables such as temperature, oxygen levels, nutrient concentrations and species composition can be manipulated in studies to ascertain their roles in the natural system.

In creating the museum's living coral reef exhibit, for example, the marine biologist demonstrated the essential role that bottom-dwelling algae play in the biologically productive shallow-water environment, a role previously understood only in general terms. In combination with waves and currents that wash over the reef, algae provide oxygen to the system and remove wastes. The plants are also a major food source for reef animals, and they produce calcium carbonate that builds the reef. Indeed, Adey's efforts to create a self-sustaining reef were unsuccessful until he could reproduce the conditions that allow the algae to carry out their life-sustaining role.

A lightweight ultrasonic telemetry tag attached across the top shell of this Atlantic blue crab enables environmental biologist Anson Hines of the Environmental Research Center to track the crab's movements after it is released into the Rhode River, a subestuary of the Chesapeake Bay. (Photo by Jeff Ploskonka)

UNDERSTANDING BIODIVERSITY

An Exploration of the Biological Richness of Our Fragile Earth

This dramatic view of the Panama Canal locks at Miraflores shows the passage of ships between the Caribbean Sea and the Pacific Ocean. The two bodies of water, separated by the isthmus of Panama, provide a unique laboratory for scientists at the Tropical Research Institute to study the development of species. (Photo by Carl Hansen)

Ross Robertson, a Tropical Research Institute research biologist, captured this exquisitely colored clarion angelfish on film during his research for a field guide to fishes of the tropical eastern Pacific.

Most residents of the Northern Hemisphere know the tropical rainforests as "jungle," a word that originally meant "wasteland." Indeed, until only recently, much of the world had dismissed one of the Earth's most prolific ecosystems as wastelands—impenetrable thickets of vegetation teeming with strange creatures.

Today, the emerald-green expanses of Latin America, West Africa, Southeast Asia and the South Pacific islands are recognized as a global lifeline. Now covering only 7 percent of the Earth's surface, about half of their original extent, tropical rainforests house at least half of the world's uncounted millions of plant and animal species. Extinction of many of these species is imminent as huge tracts of tropical forest are leveled at an alarming rate.

No one really knows the exact rate of deforestation. But all signs indicate that it is accelerating. In 1980, the United Nations estimated that, worldwide, about 28 acres of tropical forest were cut or burned each minute, resulting in an annual loss of 100,000 square miles. At the end of the decade, Thomas Lovejoy, Smithsonian assistant secretary for external affairs and chairman of the U.S. National Committee for Man and the Biosphere, calculated that, in Brazil alone, about 40 acres of virgin Amazonian forest were burned each minute. Continuing this irreversible destruction sets the stage for one of the greatest mass extinctions of all time.

For many years, Smithsonian scientists have been studying the plants and animals of tropical forests, where evolution has given rise to the most varied and most specialized forms of life. The Institution has more scientists studying the tropics than any other organization in the world. Moreover, the Smithsonian Tropical Research Institute, headquartered in Panama, is one of the leading facilities in the tropics devoted to basic biological research. Another Smithsonian bureau, the National Zoo, is pioneering the development of artificial breeding methods and techniques for preserving germ cells and embryos of threatened animals. Such measures may ultimately secure the survival of a number of endangered species. And the National Museum of Natural History has scientists working in many areas of the tropics as well.

Still, "we know more about the surface of the moon than we know about the tropics," STRI director Ira Rubinoff says. "In many cases, there are insufficient data on which to base sound management practices."

Astonishing Variety

From the forest floor to the tops of the tallest trees, reaching more than 100 feet, tropical forest ecosystems are inhabited by millions of organisms, each one a specialist genetically adapted to perform a unique role. But how prolific is life in these environments, and do the same forces operate in all tropical forests around the world, fostering similar levels of species diversity?

Current knowledge permits only vague answers to these questions. In 1980, scientists Robin Foster and Stephen Hubbell, working at the Tropical Research Institute, initiated a pioneering study that is yielding precise tabulations of tropical-tree diversity and insights into forest regeneration. Their census of a 124-acre plot of 400- to 500-year-old forest on Barro Colorado Island tallied 238,000 woody plants representing 306 species.

In collaboration with the Forest Research Institute of Malaysia, STRI scientists helped design a similar long-term study of Malaysian lowland rainforest. Results of the first census were surprising. More than 800 tree species—more species than occur in all of the United States and Canada and more than twice the number on the same-sized plot in Panama—were represented among the 320,000 trees and saplings counted. Why the two study sites differed so markedly in their species totals is the subject of continuing research. Also under study are the factors that govern the distribution, abundance and survival of individual species, information that can be used to develop sustainable forestry practices.

Using the research approach developed at STRI, India and several other countries are setting up large-scale plots to study the diversity and dynamics of their tropical forests. STRI scientists are coordinating this emerging international network of studies in the New and Old World tropics.

In all, the Earth's rainforests are estimated to contain 50,000 species of trees. Each tree species may contain insects, land crabs, birds, bats, snakes, rodents and other organisms that depend exclusively, or nearly so, on their host for survival. Eradicate just one tree species and many other organisms will also become extinct.

Firsthand observations of the intricacy of relationships among tropical species led Smithsonian entomologist Terry Erwin to conclude that the diversity of life on Earth greatly exceeds the standard estimate of 5 million to 10 million species. Erwin's "working hypothesis," based on his count of more than 1,100 species of beetles that live in just one species of tree in Panama, is that the total may ap-

proach 30 million; his further work in Amazonian Peru indicates this may be a conservative estimate.

Resulting from this research is the Smithsonian's ambitious program to catalog and study the terrestrial and aquatic species in the protected reserves of Amazonia, the world's largest and most threatened expanse of tropical forest. The Biodiversity in Latin America Program—which is called BIOLAT—launched in the late 1980s with support from the U.S. Congress and the United Nations, is the first of its kind, a standardized effort to investigate tropical forests over time.

It is an enormous task. One-fifth of the world's species are estimated to live in Amazonia, and nearly all organisms inventoried there will be "new" to science. The plants and animals will be surveyed systematically, using a grid-mapping technique developed by Erwin and others. The inventories are exhaustive; plants and animals found

Tree measurements are taken on Barro Colorado Island by Sue Williams (right) of the Tropical Research Institute and her assistants from the University of Panama as part of a five-year tree census. Projects worldwide are being modeled after this ongoing program. (Photo by Carl Hansen)

Museum of Natural History entomologist Terry Erwin uses fogging equipment to collect insect specimens, one step in the effort to inventory tropical plants and animals. Some 1,700 species can be found in a single tropical tree in Amazonia, and nearly all of them are new to science. (Photo by Chip Clark)

ternational effort to analyze the plant life of Suriname, Guyana and French Guiana—an area of tropical America that has received little botanical attention. One aim is to identify areas in the Guianas that merit protection on the basis of their biotic diversity.

Learning the Lessons of Tropical Nature

No other region of the tropics has been studied as extensively as the forested preserves under the custodianship of the Tropical Research Institute (see "A Tropical Island for Science," Page 62). There and in the coastal waters of the Atlantic and Pacific oceans, STRI scientists and visiting researchers have pieced together many lessons of nature that can be learned in the tropics.

The scope of the more than 150 STRI research projects under way at any given time is broad, ranging from the behavior of tiny "pseudo scorpions" that live under the forewings of beetles to intercontinental comparisons of tropical vegetation. From these studies emerge theories that explain the deceptive workings of evolution and its myriad biological manifestations, as well as clearer understanding of the ecological complexities of relationships between plants and animals and between environments and organisms.

"Data can be gathered in this part of the world on evolutionary puzzles that have been the subject of endless speculation," says Harilaos Lessios, a STRI expert on the evolution and ecology of marine invertebrates.

Speciation Mechanisms

Lessios and other STRI scientists have capitalized on the Tropical Research Institute's proximity to one of nature's grandest experiments, the isthmus of Panama. The isthmus arose some 3 million years ago, creating two seas from one and separating populations of marine organisms. The isolated populations embarked on separate evolutionary courses, leading to remarkably and—at this point—inexplicably different species.

Comparisons between species that live in the Pacific and those that live in the Atlantic's Caribbean Sea have provided stern challenges to the view that evolution at the genetic level proceeds at a nearly constant pace, set by a "molecular clock." Lessios' studies of sea urchins, for example, whose common ancestors parted ways when the isthmus arose, suggest that the molecular clock needs to be reset. He compared the proteins of Caribbean and Pacific sea urchins and found that they differed in

in each square meter—from the forest floor to the highest point in the canopy—are registered on laptop computers in the field. The result of the inventorying and mapping efforts is a kind of group picture, a snapshot of all the organisms that occur in a single ecosystem.

With this baseline information, scientists can go back and take another group picture. "Follow-up studies," Erwin says, "will give us information about the long-term biological cycles operative in the tropics, something we know little about."

Combined with training programs for Latin American students (see "Training Tomorrow's Scientists," Page 59), biodiversity inventories are well under way at reserves in Bolivia, Peru and Ecuador. Complementary studies are being conducted in other parts of South America. For example, Laurence Skog and other botanists from the Museum of Natural History are participating in an in-

Dawning recognition of the perils of habitat destruction has prompted calls for a major scientific effort to study rainforests and other threatened ecosystems. One aim of such an effort is to provide information essential to crafting effective conservation measures. Another is to learn as much as possible about life in imperiled ecosystems before the opportunity vanishes.

As species of plants and animals disappear from Earth—many of them without ever being studied by scientists—we lose valuable genetic resources. New foods, biological control agents and medicines are among the products that await discovery. Given the fact that about one-fourth of the medicines used in the United States today contain chemicals derived from plants, biological studies of the tropics will directly contribute to human welfare.

The motivations for studying endangered ecosystems are many, but even if there is adequate financial support, the job will not get done without enough scientists to do the work. Unfortunately, the world's complement of scientists with the necessary expertise is dwarfed by the size of the task.

Training is integrated into nearly all of the Smithsonian's major biological research programs, and many of the Institution's educational activities are geared toward bolstering the number of scientists in developing countries. At the Smithsonian Tropical Research Institute, some fellowships and internships are reserved for students and scientists from developing countries. With financial assistance from the Exxon Corp. and the Smithsonian, nearly 100 men and women from all parts of the world conduct research each year at the institute. In addition, several staff scientists hold positions at universities in Costa Rica and in the Republic of Panama.

Besides providing support for graduate and postdoctoral students, as well as visiting scientists, the National Zoo offers training courses tailored to the special needs of scientific personnel in developing countries. Each year, about 25 students from more than 10 countries participate in the wildlife conservation training course developed by National Zoo scientist Rasanayagam Rudran and held at the Zoo's Conservation and Research Center. Rudran also conducts similar courses in such countries as Venezuela, Malaysia and China. The captive management component of these courses has been developed as a complementary training program by Christen Wemmer, the Zoo's associate director for conservation and captive breeding.

Among the many training and educational activities at the National Museum of Natural History are those developed in conjunction with the museum's Biodiversity in Latin America Program. At each research site, scientists and students from host countries are directly involved in the inventorying of species and in related studies. On-site workshops are given for biology and conservation-management students, who assume greater responsibility for the project as their expertise grows.

Finally, the Smithsonian is an active participant in the United Nations Educational, Scientific and Cultural Organization's Man and the Biosphere Program. Since 1987, the Smithsonian's program, currently directed by Francisco Dallmeier, has conducted a number of training courses in Latin America. It has also developed methodology protocols for inventorying biological diversity in the tropics. The Smithsonian's tropical rainforest programs bring the Institution into worldwide collaboration with other institutions to address the critical issue of environmental degradation and, in particular, deforestation. ✱

The National Zoo's Christen Wemmer (foreground) performs a demonstration during an international wildlife training course conducted at the Zoo's Conservation and Research Center. The group includes participants from Sri Lanka, India and China. (Photo by Jessie Cohen)

composition by a factor of 20. Had these species evolved according to the constant ticking of the molecular clock over the past 3 million years, the differences in the proteins—and, consequently, in the genes that encode them—would have been far less striking. The disparity between the molecular-clock theory and the results of studies by Lessios and other STRI scientists indicates that important steps in the evolutionary process remain to be discovered.

The substantial differences between the Caribbean and Pacific organisms that descended from common ancestors stem from geographic isolation. Such isolation reduces or eliminates exchange of genetic material between populations, thereby creating the opportunity for divergence between populations and, on occasion, the evolution of new species. Nearly all explanations of animal evolution entail a similar scenario.

STRI researchers have proposed another possible speciation mechanism, based on sexual behavior. Mary Jane West-Eberhard and William Eberhard, STRI researchers working in Costa Rica, argue that sexual selection is an important agent of biological diversity. In many animal species, males compete for mates. The two biologists have suggested that the responses of females—their selection of mates based on the shape and structure of male genitalia and other elaborate morphology and signaling behavior—are the driving force behind the evolution of complex and species-specific male traits, including genital morphology.

In some instances, the scientists contend, sexual selection could facilitate the origin of new species by accelerating divergence in these traits. Another frequent product of competition—alternative strategies of resource acquisition—may also contribute to the diversity of species by providing the initial elaboration of novel behaviors.

Tropical Vegetation

In the temperate climates of the United States, we await the burst of autumn color that precedes winter and then eagerly anticipate the new buds of spring. But in the tropics and subtropics, each plant species, to paraphrase Henry David Thoreau, seems to march to a different beat. Responding to unknown clues, tropical plants shed their leaves,

Smithsonian-Tupo, a small island in the San Blas Archipelago, land of the Kuna Indians, is the home of one of the marine labs of the Tropical Research Institute. (Photo by Carl Hansen)

THE SMITHSONIAN INSTITUTION: A WORLD OF DISCOVERY

grow new ones and develop flowers according to individual rhythms. These rhythms, in turn, seem to set the cadence that governs the lives of many animal species.

On two 5-acre plots of forest, STRI scientist S. Joseph Wright has deliberately sought to interfere with the timing of plant cycles by eliminating the most noticeable climatic clues: distinct wet and dry seasons. Using irrigation equipment, Wright kept the soil in the plots near saturation during five successive dry seasons. Despite this dramatic change, the leafing and flowering patterns of most canopy and midstory tree species did not change.

Using new instruments and analytical methods, recent STRI studies have documented how some plant species have adapted to the annual dry season and explained why irrigation did not dramatically alter reproduction and growth. Wright, STRI biologist Alan Smith and visiting scientist Steve Mulkey found that some understory shrubs produce wet-season leaves that lose water rapidly and dry-season leaves that minimize water loss while maintaining similar rates of photosynthesis.

STRI researchers also study the interactions between plants and animals, finding that benefits flow both ways. Animal populations wax and wane with seed and fruit production of certain tree species. Populations of red-tailed squirrels and agoutis (a type of rodent), for example, decline when production of certain tree seeds is low. For both animals, the seeds of the palm, *Astrocaryum,* are an alternative food source. The palm, in turn, relies on agoutis for survival. STRI biologist Nicholas Smythe found that the palm's seeds will not survive to germinate unless buried by the rodents.

Ecological Disturbances

Researchers and conservationists are challenged today with untangling the consequences of disruptive natural forces from the damage caused by careless human activity. Another challenge is to develop sustainable land uses that allow people to profit from the resources of tropical forests without doing irreversible harm.

Benefiting from years of extensive monitoring of environmental conditions on Barro Colorado Island, on neighboring lands and in surrounding waters, STRI researchers have added considerably to the scientific understanding of cause and effect in

---

BREAKING OCEAN WAVES SPEED GROWTH

In the search for alternatives to fossil fuels, some individuals have advocated harnessing the tremendous power released by breaking ocean waves. Do biological communities exploit this energy?

STRI ecologist Egbert Leigh and his colleagues have documented surprisingly high levels of biological productivity among intertidal organisms. In a study of the rocky, wind-swept shores of Tatoosh Island off the coast of Washington state, they found that the areas most exposed to the force of breaking waves were most crowded with organisms. Up to 98 percent of the surface of these wavebeaten areas was covered with plants and animals.

This study was inspired by Leigh's curiosity. He had frequently observed that growth in intertidal kelp communities was most luxuriant where waves beat hardest. Further work

found that wave-beaten shores supported a far higher production, and a far greater extent of frond ("leaf") surface per unit area of ground, than did tropical rainforests. Tropical forests benefit from the strong tropical sun and the absence of winter, but what, Leigh wondered, permits intertidal organisms to thrive in their fogbound, wave-pounded environment where growth is possible for only half the year? Can intertidal organisms somehow use the raw energy of breaking waves?

Leigh calculated that waves deliver 15 times more energy per year to the shores of this northeastern Pacific island than does the sun. He and his colleagues compiled productivity estimates for organisms—sea palms, shrubby kelps and mussels—found primarily in wave-beaten sites. For the sea palms and shrubby kelps, an-

nual levels of vegetative growth (pounds of dry matter produced per square foot of rock) were two to five times greater than for most rainforests. Even mussels, which acquire energy by consuming other organisms, produce annually as much dry matter per square foot as a rainforest.

These intertidal organisms do not transform wave power directly into energy. Rather, they thrive because waves continually knock off predators or restrict their activities. Breaking waves also promote photosynthesis by dividing light more evenly among fronds. The fronds of sea palms and wave-beaten kelps are continually tossed about, so that most fronds receive frequent flashes of sunlight. In contrast, light is shared much less evenly among the leaves of a forest, where ground-herbs are only rarely lighted by sun flecks. ✺

Since 1946, scientists at the Smithsonian Tropical Research Institute have been scrutinizing nearly every square inch of the Barro Colorado Nature Monument—a 4,000-acre island, formed in 1913 as a result of damming the Chagres River during construction of the Panama Canal, and a preserve of 9,500 acres of forest on nearby peninsulas.

On Barro Colorado, scientists have tallied 1,369 species of plants, more than those in all of Europe. They have also documented 366 species of birds, five species of monkeys, 56 species of bats, 30 species of frogs, 22 species of lizards, 40 species of snakes, 300 species of butterflies and 200 species of ants. Over the span of more than a decade, STRI scientists have tracked hourly changes in environmental conditions— temperature, wind speed and direction, water salinity levels—on the island and at a neighboring tropical reef.

The result of these and other efforts is the most detailed picture of tropical nature available. But this still-unfolding picture is only a means to a very difficult end: to explain how nature has created this biological richness. Why do 2½ acres on the island hold as many as 175 species of canopy trees, while a plot of the same size in the richest temperate-zone forest contains only about 75?

In a given year, STRI researchers and more than 200 visiting scientists tackle variations of this question. During the more than four decades of STRI's stewardship of the biological preserve, some 2,000 studies have examined the ecology, behavior and evolution of tropical plants and animals, and the past and present impacts of human activities on tropical nature.

To support its comprehensive program, STRI has research facilities on Barro Colorado; on Naos Island, located along Panama's Pacific coast; at

Punta Galeta, site of a fringing coral reef in the Caribbean Sea; on a tiny cay in the San Blas Archipelago, a string of 300 Caribbean islands stretching from Panama to Colombia; and in a wet forest on a mountain in western Panama. In Panama City, STRI's new Tupper Research and Conference Center features laboratories for specialized investigations, as well as an auditorium and other facilities for scientific meetings.

STRI interprets its research mission broadly. Though most studies focus on the ecosystems under the institute's care, STRI scientists and their collaborators address biological questions that span the tropical world. During a typical year, STRI staff members and their associates conduct research in about 40 countries. Together, these efforts are providing a global scientific perspective on tropical biodiversity and on the complex issues stemming from the destruction of rainforests and other fragile ecosystems. ✳

A 100-foot-high crane looming above the rainforest in Panama's Parque Metropolitano lowers scientists Alan Smith of the Tropical Research Institute and Geoffrey Parker of the Environmental Research Center to different levels of the canopy for measuring temperature and humidity. (Photo by Carl Hansen)

Opposite: These dart-poison frogs, little more than half an inch long, are among the diverse species found in Panama and studied by research scientist Stanley Rand at the Tropical Research Institute. (Photo by Carl Hansen)

A dark oil slick from a 1986 crude oil spill encroaches on coastal ecosystems near Galeta, Panama, where Tropical Research Institute scientists had earlier compiled base-line data. (Photo by Carl Hansen)

lations of a once-dominant coral species, but inflicted little damage on populations of predator and competitor organisms. In fact, the predators are relatively more abundant now than before the storm. As a result, the populations of the once-dominant type of coral continued to decline years after the hurricane, suggesting that the composition of the coral reef may be unpredictable.

Ironically, recovery of coral populations may depend on the uncertain status of a predator: the long-spined sea urchin of the genus *Diadema*. In 1983, a disease outbreak killed 99 percent of all *Diadema,* which feed on algae. The herbivore's nearly complete demise, however, has disproportionately benefited algae, which reproduce so prolifically that they are overgrowing and "smothering" live coral. Knowlton has found that algae now cover 90 percent of some segments of Jamaican reefs; live coral covers only 5 percent.

Human-caused disturbances can be as devastating as natural catastrophes. In 1986, a spill of more than 2 million gallons of crude oil fouled the mangrove forests, coral reefs, seagrass beds and intertidal flats east of the Caribbean entrance to the Panama Canal. Although a disaster by any measure, the spill also provided a rare opportunity to examine the effects of oil pollution, because some of the damaged habitats had been studied during the previous 20 years by researchers at STRI's Galeta Marine Laboratory.

In a long-term project led by STRI scientists Jeremy Jackson and Brian Keller, an international team of researchers has been scrutinizing the spill's impacts since the oil first began polluting coastal ecosystems near Galeta. Results place the devastation and complexity of effects on a scale comparable to that of damage by powerful hurricanes.

Within a few months, mangrove trees were killed along 17 miles of coastline. Although the oiled sites are showing signs of new growth, it may take two or three decades for the regrowth of trees to mature fully. In each of the three types of mangrove-dominated habitat, populations of all major organisms attached to prop roots dropped steeply, and recovery of mussels, oysters and other organisms has been variable but slow. Damage along the shoreline was expected, but other impacts documented by the STRI team contradict the findings of previous oil-spill studies and laboratory experiments. Earlier work, for instance, suggested that submerged coral reefs and seagrass beds suffer minor damage from oil pollution. In contrast, Jackson, Keller and their colleagues documented significant subtidal damage, and coral populations have not recovered.

nature. On the regularly surveyed, 124-acre plot of forest on the island, scientists found that 16 percent of the trees died in the five-year period between 1980–1981 and 1985–1986. The annual mortality rate during the five-year span averaged more than 3 percent, or about three times higher than the previously estimated rate. The researchers attribute the increase to the severe drought caused by the 1982–1983 El Niño, the cyclical warming of a broad band of water in the Pacific. During the prolonged dry spell, an estimated 10 percent of the trees died. Results of the next tree census should reveal whether the damaging effects of the drought persist in longer periods of time.

In the Caribbean, STRI scientists are monitoring the effects of two natural phenomena. In 1980, Hurricane Allen devastated coral reefs off the north coast of Jamaica. As documented by STRI biologist Nancy Knowlton, the hurricane decimated popu-

A Hedge Against Extinction

Threatened.... Endangered.... Extinct. This is the grim litany of habitat destruction. As their natural ranges are reduced to ever-smaller parcels, populations of plant and animal species are brought ever closer to extinction. Populations of many species have already dropped to dangerously low levels; continuing habitat destruction will add new entries to the list of threatened and endangered species.

Joining with other organizations, the National Zoo is helping to preserve populations of animals in the wild and, in some instances their only hope, in zoos and aquariums. The National Zoo's wide-ranging research programs—at the 163-acre park in Washington, the 3,100-acre Conservation and Research Center in Front Royal, Va., and at sites around the world—reflect not only the magnitude of the need, but also the complexity of species conservation.

NZP scientists play lead roles in the management of seven species on national and international lists of endangered animals. They also contribute to conservation and propagation efforts focused on the small populations of 21 other species, including tigers and one-horned rhinoceroses.

From such specialties as veterinary medicine and pathology, the NZP research program has expanded to encompass nearly all fields of biology: endocrinology, nutrition, animal behavior, ecology, evolutionary biology, population and molecular genetics, reproductive physiology, and functional morphology and energetics. Research results translate into improvements in the well-being of the more than 4,000 animals (representing 470 species) at the Zoo's Washington facility and the approximately 800 animals (40 species) at the Conservation and Research Center. Moreover, each research finding—reported in the 100 papers published annually by NZP scientists, research associates and graduate students—has the potential to increase a species' survival prospects.

"These efforts cannot save species on the scale that will be needed if habitat destruction continues," Zoo director Michael Robinson says, "but they are positive signs. We can save an occasional 'Rembrandt' or 'Botticelli' among the threatened animals, but it is physically impossible to save the majority of nature's masterworks."

Christen Wemmer, associate director for conservation and captive breeding programs, looks over the National Zoo's Conservation and Research Center in Front Royal, Va. (Photo by Jessie Cohen)

Cause for Hope: The Golden Lion Tamarin

Success, it is said, has many owners. This adage certainly applies in the case of a comprehensive NZP-led program to reintroduce captive-bred golden lion tamarins to their remaining natural habitat in the coastal rainforests of Brazil.

The golden lion tamarin, a squirrel-size primate with a luxurious gold-to-orange mane, is in desperate straits. The animal has become nearly extinct in the wild because of forest clearing for agriculture and because of the illegal trade in exotic pets.

In 1983, when scientists began studies in Brazil, only 200 golden lion tamarins remained there. Even fewer tamarins lived in zoos.

Today, the situation is improving. Some 600 tamarins have been raised in zoos and, after years of painstaking research, 89 have been reintroduced in Brazil as part of the cooperative Golden Lion Tamarin Conservation Program.

In addition, ownership of all golden lion tamarins living in zoos was recently given to the people of Brazil. Conservation and education efforts in Brazil during the past seven years have contributed greatly to the chances for the survival of tamarins—and many other species that share their habitat. In fact, the project's underlying goal has been to preserve the habitat for the myriad mammals, birds and invertebrates that live in the coastal rainforest, says Dr. Benjamin Beck, asso-

ciate director for biological programs at the National Zoo.

The conservation program was initiated by National Zoo scientists in 1972. They learned, first, how to breed the tamarins successfully and, then, how to reintroduce them to the wild. But the wild in this case—the coastal rainforest—has shrunk by 98 percent since 1650.

Fortunately, a fragile island of rainforest, the Poco das Antas Biological Reserve, still exists 60 miles northeast of Rio de Janeiro. The reserve—12,000 acres of forest, swamp and grassland—is a lifeboat for the tamarins. "The golden lion tamarin would be extinct in the wild today if not for the creation of this reserve," Beck says emphatically.

Near Poco das Antas, two tamarin families from North America—Jenny, Maria, Carlos, Pedro and Pablo, along with Celia, Marty, Maude and Melvin—have been introduced to two males who have survived the travails of forest life. Beck and others hope that these male tamarins will each form a group with one of the reintroduced groups and that the males will pass on their survival skills—avoiding predators, foraging and choosing nest sites—to the newcomers.

Beck calls this reintroduction method the "veteran/greenhorn" technique. He is studying the procedure as a possible improvement over the method of simply releasing tamarins that are naive about the rigors of forest survival.

This captive-born golden lion tamarin, after being introduced into the Atlantic coastal forest of Brazil, wears a radio transmitter that aids in follow-up monitoring of the project carried out by the National Zoo. (Photo by Jessie Cohen)

Goodbye zoo. Hello BioPark. Since the mid-1980s, National Zoological Park director Michael Robinson has been crusading for a new kind of zoo, one that is not a zoo at all, at least by conventional standards. Robinson, a biologist with extensive research experience in the tropics, advocates a natural, final step in the direction already taken by most zoos. He is proposing to transform the Smithsonian's *zoological* park into a *biological* park. The BioPark will combine elements of existing zoos, aquariums, natural history museums, botanic gardens, arboretums and ethnological/anthropological museums to create a holistic form of "bioexhibitry."

Essentially, a bioexhibit would portray life in all its interconnectedness. Creating the BioPark means ending a whole series of unnatural separations. It means exhibiting plants and animals, not plants or animals (as in botanic gardens and zoos).

It also means that aquatic organisms belong in the same exhibition complex as terrestrial organisms. Exhibits on comparative structures, life functions and the history of life on Earth belong inseparably with exhibits of living plants and animals.

In "Amazonia," a major new "bioexhibit" at the National Zoo, visitors gain a new perspective of life in the tropics, one of the world's richest ecosystems. In exchange for enduring—briefly—the heat and humidity of the Amazon rainforest, visitors experience the complexity and interdependence of life at three levels of this ecosystem: forest canopy, forest floor and river.   ✱

Horticulturists lower a 15,000-pound mahogany tree into the "Amazonia" exhibition during its construction at the National Zoo. In this new "bioexhibit," visitors experience the sights and sounds of the complex ecosystem of an Amazon rainforest and learn about Smithsonian research being conducted there. (Photo by Jessie Cohen)

The first American flamingo born at the National Zoo hatched in June 1992, the result of a successful research program on reproduction. (Photo by Jessie Cohen)

"Before reintroduction of tamarins was possible, we needed a zoo population breeding successfully enough that we could have 'surplus' animals to return to the wild," says Dr. Devra Kleiman, the Zoo's assistant director for research. "In 1973, the situation in zoos was bleak. We had fighting within groups, nutritional problems and low reproduction rates, as well as high mortality rates among those few infants that were born." At that time, she explains, tamarins were kept in large groups of breeding-age animals along with their offspring.

Kleiman had a hunch, however, that keeping the animals in large groups was the problem. Her previous work included research on dogs, wolves and rodents. Most of these animals are monogamous, forming pairs with exclusive reproductive access to one another for extended periods of time. Although this trait is unusual among primates, she concluded that golden lion tamarins also practice monogamy.

Kleiman and her colleagues also discovered the importance of keeping young tamarins around their parents as the next set of young are raised. "Tamarin adolescents become involved in infant care because the 2½-ounce infants grow quickly and become a major burden on the mother after about the first week," she says. In turn, the social and parental experience adolescents gain is indispensable for their survival as adults.

With the mystery solved, the animals began to breed successfully. It became necessary, though, to expand the tamarin gene pool beyond one zoo. Kleiman pioneered a system in which researchers at a number of zoos agreed to breed and manage their separate groups of tamarins as one population, further reducing problems associated with inbreeding, such as high infant mortality rates.

By 1983, sufficient numbers of tamarins existed for the scientists to consider reintroduction. But the Poco das Antas reserve was at capacity in terms of the numbers of golden lion tamarins it could support. The next step, then, was to enlist the help of landowners adjacent to the reserve to find new sites where zoo-bred animals could be released.

To date, about 2,000 acres have been committed—a 15 percent increase in the area of the Poco das Antas reserve. "Thousands of additional acres will be needed," Kleiman says. "The tamarins need space to find unrelated mates and avoid inbreeding."

Since 1984, more than 50 offspring of reintroduced tamarins have been born in the wild and about 60 percent have survived. One released male even managed to find his way into the life of a wild tamarin and, together, they produced two additional offspring.

Perils That Small Populations Face

If the population of any endangered species dips below a certain critical size, even the most elaborate of propagation programs may not offset the devastating effects of inbreeding. That critical number is not known with certainty; rather, it depends on the species and a variety of genetic and demographic factors.

A goal for Jonathan Ballou, NZP's population manager, is to develop statistical techniques for estimating the minimum viable population for species in the wild and for those in zoos. Ballou, NZP research biologist Katherine Ralls and a colleague from Washington University tabulated the "costs" of inbreeding in 40 populations of captive animals representing 38 species. In all but four populations, matings between parents and their offspring or between siblings reduced the survival of young. On average, the survival of offspring produced by these matings was only two-thirds that of offspring produced by matings of unrelated animals.

NZP scientists are also studying the genetic diversity of dwindling populations of species in native habitats. In research on cheetahs, nature's fastest mammal, NZP reproductive physiologist David Wildt and Stephen O'Brien, a researcher at the National Cancer Institute, found unexpectedly high levels of genetic uniformity in the wild felines. Predictably, the lack of diversity has had damaging consequences. Reproduction levels are low and infant mortality is high. Wildt, O'Brien and their colleagues are conducting similar studies of koalas in Australia and lions in Asia and Africa.

Saving Diversity

The remnant populations of cheetahs, pumas, clouded leopards, certain tigers and several other species of wild cats are moving ever closer to the critical-size threshold. In contrast, a distant relative of these animals—the domestic cat—is flourishing to the point of overabundance. Yet, when NZP researchers succeeded in producing "test-tube" domestic kittens, they made an important stride in the effort to save the world's endangered felines.

In fact, this accomplishment by Wildt and his associates marked the first time a carnivorous animal was produced by in-vitro fertilization. The next step is to try the technique on wild cats, a task complicated by the physiological peculiarities of each species.

NZP scientists were also called on to assist in a crash effort to save the Florida panther, a subspecies of puma reduced to about 25 individuals. Wildt and a graduate student, Ann Miller, first tested their "test-tube" methods on a related animal, the Colorado cougar. Fertilization occurred in about half of 70 eggs mixed with sperm. And of the fertilized eggs, 10 underwent the initial cell divisions of embryo development, a promising indication that the technique may eventually be successful for the pumas.

The fate of another highly endangered species,

the black-footed ferret, also hinges on the work of NZP and other scientists. The animal was the casualty of misguided efforts to control prairie dogs, the wild ferret's primary prey. Western ranchers poisoned prairie dog communities in the mistaken belief they could save grass for grazing livestock. Black-footed ferrets were considered extinct until 18 animals were discovered in Wyoming in 1981.

These ferrets may also be spared extinction through NZP research on domestic ferrets. In a technique known as laparoscopy, Zoo scientists used a fiber-optic system to deposit sperm in female domestic ferrets. The artificial insemination procedure has achieved a conception rate of 70 percent and the live births of more than 100 kits. Equally important, Dr. JoGayle Howard of the Zoo demonstrated that ferret semen could be frozen and stored for more than a year without damage and then utilized for successful artificial insemination. This means that researchers might have another way to avoid inbreeding; after several generations have passed, ferret semen can be thawed and used to impregnate females that are genetically distant from the donor male.

Research on artificial insemination and in-vitro fertilization methods for animals is still in its infancy. The exceptions are farm animals (and humans), but early on, biologists discovered that procedures developed for domesticated animals do not transfer directly to other species. As a result, researchers must carry out a battery of behavioral and biological studies on each species before devising fertilization strategies. Often, basic information, such as when the females of a species ovulate, is unknown. These facts must be gleaned with as little disruption to the animals as possible. Success depends on the contributions of many scientists.

For some species, artificial breeding methods under development may be their last defense against extinction. Their last preserve of genetic diversity may be the eggs, sperm and embryos preserved by other scientific methods. As long as this germplasm exists, hope remains that endangered species can persist in captivity and in the wild.

In addition to refining "cryopreservation" techniques, in which reproductive cells and embryos are frozen and stored in liquid nitrogen, NZP scientists are investigating other preservation options. Building on these advances, the Zoo hopes to develop and coordinate a Genetic Resource Bank, an international repository of genetic diversity. Conservationists agree that artificial breeding will be an important tool for managing and sustaining populations of endangered animals.

LEARNING

FROM

THE PAST

A Chronicle of Our History,
from Earliest Humans to
Our Postindustrial Society

The Smithsonian tradition of Arctic research continues with excavations at Kamaiyuk site, an early Inuit winter village near Kodlunarn Island, base camp of 16th-century British explorer Martin Frobisher, off Baffin Island in the Canadian Arctic. The site contains English tile, coal, flint and other materials obtained by the Inuit from the Frobisher expedition. (Photo by William Fitzhugh)

This Arapaho ghost dance dress from Oklahoma was one of a hundred objects selected by American Indians for the 1992–1993 "Pathways of Tradition" exhibition at the Museum of the American Indian in New York City. The objects represented a cross section of Indian culture and creativity and were but a sample of the museum's 1 million-artifact collection. (Photo by Karen Furth)

An organization as large and popular as the Smithsonian is bound to have acquired at least a few labels over the years. None captures the full range of the Institution's mission and accomplishments. Neither "university on the Mall" nor "window on the world," neither "keeper of the past" nor even the venerable "U.S. National Museum" quite encompasses the Smithsonian's strategy to secure evidence of the chronicle of human and natural history—to preserve it, to study it and to interpret the past to the present.

Somewhere along the line, the Smithsonian acquired the affectionate but mischievously misleading nickname of "the nation's attic," a facile sobriquet that fails on all levels. The relics are not collected accidentally, whimsically or haphazardly. They are selected for their exemplary quality to represent what becomes lost in time. They are painstakingly preserved as the only and best evidence of themselves, against which any copy or description must be measured for fidelity. They are preserved not merely that we may know of them, but so we can see and touch them, perhaps even hear, smell and taste them, and display them to show what we believe the past to have been like. They are the means of acquiring new knowledge.

When the topic of study is the one that is endlessly interesting to humans—humans themselves—archaeological and cultural artifacts are indispensable. Whether these are pottery shards, written correspondence or paraphernalia from past political campaigns, records of the human past always fascinate and always illuminate. Archaeological, anthropological and historical research helps us to understand ourselves and the nature of human interactions—good and bad—during the hundreds of thousands of years that modern *Homo sapiens* has been on the planet. Such research provides perspectives on the past that become lenses for viewing the present. These studies can expose progress and mistakes, often simultaneously.

Many staff people at the Smithsonian study the development of human culture and human societies, beginning with the evolution of modern humans and extending to the present. Hundreds of other scholars come to the Institution each year to use its unparalleled resources for studying human history. Only a few chapters in this part of the Smithsonian story of discovery—the human legacy—can be highlighted here.

Early Human History

Distant biological relatives of humans are known as far back as 4 million years ago. In the context of 3.5 billion years of biological evolution, however, the emergence of our ancestors is a recent development. A 1,000-page chronological discussion of life on Earth would devote only the final page to our line of descent. And on this last page, the species *Homo sapiens* would be the subject of a brief concluding sentence.

This last page, particularly the last sentence, has proven to be extremely difficult to write, however. The opening phrase on the origin of the human species has been written and rewritten, but never to the complete satisfaction of everyone, nor to anyone for very long.

Of course, early human history could never be reduced to a single sentence. There are too many fascinating episodes. Evolution of our species is the obvious starting point. But the complexity and diversity of modern *Homo sapiens* and our ubiquitous presence on the planet inspire many other questions about the past: How did early humans spread from their origins in Africa to nearly all areas of the globe? How did societies develop and what held them together? Why did great civilizations arise and then vanish? Ultimately, we would like to understand the common heritage of humankind, as well as the sources of such great cultural diversity.

This is the collective goal of researchers in the Department of Anthropology at the National Museum of Natural History and others elsewhere at the Smithsonian. They pursue this goal from many angles. The department's physical anthropologists study human remains to decipher human evolution, to describe life in ancient societies, to uncover the origins and biological significance of certain human diseases and to trace the distribution of prehistoric peoples (see "Clues to Mysteries of Prehistory and Modern Medicine," Page 74). Cultural anthropologists study individual societies—their organization and structure, their way of life, their language and other aspects of their culture. Archaeologists systematically recover and study the material remains of past societies as part of an effort to reconstruct past cultures.

Landscape of Human Evolution

Recent studies suggest that the first modern humans appeared in sub-Saharan Africa between 200,000 and 500,000 years ago. The challenge of pinning down exactly when our species arose and determining the identity of our immediate ances-

Research assistant Lassa Skinner (left) records data at a Museum of Natural History dig at Olorgesailie, Kenya. The excavation is uncovering an extinct species of elephant that existed in the early human ancestor community about 1.1 million years ago. (Photo by Richard Potts)

tors has occupied paleoanthropologists for more than a century. Scant attention, however, has been paid to two related and intriguing questions: How and why did *Homo sapiens,* arguably the planet's dominant species, evolve?

Capitalizing on advanced techniques for dating specimens and other analytical methods, the Smithsonian's Human Origins Program works toward answering these questions. Research is under way at Olorgesailie, a unique site in southern Kenya. With colleagues from other institutions, physical anthropologist Richard Potts, paleobiologist Anna Behrensmeyer and geologist William Melson have determined that human ancestors lived in the ancient lake basin there over a million-year span—from about 1.1 million years ago to the present. During this important but little-studied period, preliminary evidence suggests that there was separation of hominid groups from commu-

Some 8,000 years ago, the Indians who inhabited the southern coast of present-day Ecuador met their food needs by hunting, fishing and gathering. Life was simple and short; life expectancy at birth was only 25 years. Over the succeeding millennia, the ways of modern society evolved. Coastal Indians clustered in ever-larger communities, relied increasingly on agriculture for their food needs and—compared with their ancestors—led more sedentary lives.

But in many ways, the path of social evolution did not lead to a better life, according to Douglas Ubelaker, a physical anthropologist in the National Museum of Natural History who has studied human remains recovered from nine sites in Ecuador. Between about 6000 B.C. and A.D. 1700, infant and child mortality increased, while the lifespans of adults increased only slightly. Moreover, the incidence of anemia, dental caries and infectious diseases rose over time. Ubelaker hypothesizes that these were the biological consequences of a cultural transformation that might, by other measures, be called progress. His studies suggest

that settlement in larger communities was accompanied by poor nutrition, increased stress and more chances for contracting diseases.

Ubelaker's studies are but one example of what can be learned from scientific investigations of human remains. Often, in fact, these remains are the only means to learn about prehistoric peoples, offering insights into human societies—their diets, disease problems and ways of life—over thousands of years. Equally important, by tracking the occurrence of specific diseases within and among populations over time, the Smithsonian's physical anthropologists are contributing to modern medicine's efforts to understand such afflictions as osteoporosis, rheumatoid arthritis, tuberculosis and syphilis.

The Natural History Museum's collection of 34,000 human remains (few are complete skeletons, and nearly all have been collected in archaeological excavations or in salvage operations at such places as construction projects) is a resource of increasing scientific value. New and emerging techniques that study proteins and DNA are helping researchers extract ever more detailed in-

formation on an increasing number of anthropological and medical questions. Recognizing this important opportunity, the Smithsonian's Conservation Analytical Laboratory, in collaboration with the Museum of Natural History and other organizations, has launched a major effort to extend the analytical methods of molecular biology and other fields to applications in physical anthropology.

The promise of these techniques is enormous, considering the substantial amount of information already generated by the many scientists who study the collection. For example, the museum's Donald Ortner, co-author of *Identification of Pathological Conditions in Human Skeletal Remains,* the definitive work in the field, uncovered important new information about the origins of syphilis. Scientists are engaged in a lively debate regarding the geographical origin of the disease. Ortner has identified distinctive syphilislike lesions in pre-Columbian Native American remains. He is currently looking for similar cases in Old World remains.

Ortner, whose research interests range from paleopathology—the study of ancient disease—to human evolution, describes the Institution's collection as priceless. "The men, women and children of past civilizations," he says, "often had little to leave posterity that would tell us what their lives were really like. But they did leave us their bones, and we should not waste that gift." ✻

Anthropologist Donald Ortner holds a skull from Gabon, Africa, that shows signs of chronic infection. Information on selected disease patterns in ancient pathological specimens in the Museum of Natural History's extensive skeletal collections has been computerized by Ortner and research assistant Janet Beck. (Photo by Dane Penland)

nities of carnivorous animals, which previously had co-existed as predators in the same territory.

In the long-term research program at Olorgesailie and in related studies, the Smithsonian team is establishing the context for human evolution. Initial efforts are focusing on reconstructing the environmental landscape—the topography, the climate, and the plant and animal communities—that characterized the site 1.1 million years ago. Evidence of hominid activities is then examined in light of the early human ancestors' surroundings. Moving forward in time, the researchers will be able to assess how hominids responded to opportunities and challenges as a result of changes in environmental conditions.

Since the program began in 1986, the researchers have made several important discoveries. At one excavation site, they found the nearly complete skeleton of an extinct elephant and, with it, sharp stone flakes that most probably were wielded by hominids when they butchered the carcass. Nearby, the team has also found a more upland area with a dense accumulation of animal bones and stone artifacts. The site may have been a home base for ancient hunter-gatherers, or it may have been a prime location for foraging by hominids. In this same area, the investigators also have uncovered nearly complete fossilized skeletons of hyenas and a smaller carnivore, as well as the skull and other bones of an extinct form of zebra, all of which were buried in collapsed burrows or dens that were dug into the ancient land surface.

Though these and other excavations hold important clues about the activities of early human ancestors, each yields only a glimpse, and the geological strata at Olorgesailie offer the opportunity to get a much broader view. The Smithsonian team has identified a nearly 1½-mile-long strip of undisturbed, 1.1-million-year-old ancient soil and lake sediment exposed by erosion. The researchers' unique exploration strategy calls for systematic sampling of the entire preserved landscape. With this approach, they are not only likely to uncover other sites rich with fossils, artifacts and clues to environmental conditions, but they also will be able to assess the range of hominid activities over a significant portion of the ancient habitat.

Life in the New World

About half of the Anthropology Department's 30 resident specialists concentrate on the histories of peoples in the so-called New World. Geographically, the domain of New World studies stretches across the entire Western Hemisphere. In Central and South America, research projects range from investigations of ancient Mayan culture to studies of prehistoric inhabitants of Panama and research among isolated peoples who live in the region's rainforests and whose cultures are threatened by encroaching agricultural development.

In the Arctic, scientists are reconstructing the histories of the circumpolar region's native peoples. Thus, anthropologist William Fitzhugh, director of the museum's Center for Arctic Studies, has helped trace the distribution of Eskimo and Indian cultures over a 10,000-year period in Labrador. He has also worked on the origins of Eskimo art in Alaska.

The Smithsonian tradition of Arctic research is more than a century old. But the fact that the region's cultural history remains largely unexplored reflects both the richness of that history and the political tensions that have prevented the international collaboration the subject requires. Parts of the Arctic—now divided among eight nations—have been inhabited for more than 20 millennia. Comprising 10 percent of the globe, the entire region offers an unmatched opportunity to study human relationships with the environment.

Now there are signs that the history of the Arctic and its peoples will receive the international attention they merit. One visible sign was "Crossroads of Continents: Cultures of Siberia and Alaska," an exhibition prepared by researchers from the Smithsonian and other museums in the United States, Canada and Russia. Over a six-year period, the exhibition, which debuted at the National Museum of Natural History in 1988, was shown in both the United States and Canada. The cooperative research effort leading to the exhibitions has resulted in an international network of researchers devoted to studying the cultural histories of the diverse peoples of the Arctic.

The First Americans

A more comprehensive anthropological research program in the Arctic may eventually solve the enigma of the origins of the first Americans. This question has interested paleo-Indian archaeologist Dennis Stanford since his high-school days in Wyoming. On mountain hikes, Stanford would occasionally find the sharp stone points of spears brandished 11,000 years ago by Ice Age hunters now called the Clovis people.

As a scientist at the Natural History Museum, Stanford is a leading figure in studies of the earliest known people in the lower 48 states. He has excavated several Clovis sites, in addition to sites

their elongated, leaf-shaped tips and fluted bases, have been recovered in every state in the continental United States and in Latin America.

The widespread dispersal of these masterfully crafted points compounds the mystery of the Clovis people. The handful of important archaeological sites discovered suggest that they had a short tenure in the Western Hemisphere.

"Were these people the first Americans, or were there already people here, and did the superior Clovis technology simply spread across an existing population?" Stanford asks. "All of the dated Clovis sites fall within a couple hundred years of one another. Could a population expand through North and South America that rapidly?"

Studies of the Clovis people are part of a broad spectrum of Smithsonian research devoted to Native American peoples. From the beginning of the Smithsonian's history in the mid-19th century, the Institution's archaeologists and anthropologists— ethnologists, physical anthropologists and linguists—have worked to document and preserve the cultural history of North American Indians. Today, the Natural History Museum and the Smithsonian's newly created National Museum of the American Indian together have the most comprehensive collections of American Indian artifacts in the world—several million objects in all. The centerpiece of the National Museum of the American Indian is nearly 1 million objects formerly belonging to the Museum of the American Indian, Heye Foundation in New York City. These collections, coupled with Native American collections at the National Museum of American History, the National Museum of American Art and the National Portrait Gallery, span the hemisphere, from the Arctic to Tierra del Fuego, from prehistoric time to the present day.

In addition, the majority of records in the National Anthropological Archives pertains to the native peoples of the Western Hemisphere. The collection consists of more than 200,000 photographs and nearly 2 million pages of unpublished materials on Indian ethnography, language, literature and history, used by Smithsonian researchers and others, including Native American researchers and tribal representatives. The anthropological archives is also a major resource for the Natural History Museum's Handbook of North American Indians project, an encyclopedic examination of the anthropology, history and linguistics of the continent's tribes. When completed, the 20-volume series will include the contributions of more than 1,000 experts.

Using these combined resources, researchers are

Paleo-Indian archaeologist Dennis Stanford of the Museum of Natural History has replicated prehistoric tools that were made for hunting, butchering and manufacturing. Details of early human activities are deduced by studying how these tools were made and used. (Photo by Chip Clark)

linked to other early Americans, and his novel research methods—Stanford and his colleagues once used replicas of Ice Age stone tools to butcher an elephant that had died at a Boston zoo—have contributed much to the understanding of the lifestyles of these ancient people.

Evidence amassed by Stanford and other researchers suggests the ancestral origins of the Clovis people. "Their tools and use of red ochre [a pigment prepared from iron ore] strike us as similar to archaeological sites in eastern Siberia and seem to confirm an Asian origin," Stanford explains. "We do not know, though, when they crossed the Bering Land Bridge," the huge exposed floor of the Bering Sea that linked Siberia and Alaska until about 14,000 years ago. Searches in Alaska have failed to uncover artifacts linked to the Clovis people or to their direct predecessors. In contrast, Clovis weapons points, distinctive for

piecing together a more accurate picture of the lives of the first Americans. Among the projects under way at the research branch of the National Museum of the American Indian in New York is one dealing with the famed but widely misunderstood Apache peoples.

The Apache became the focus of American attention during the 1870s when the U.S. military launched a drive to gather the various Apache tribes and confine them to reservations. Resistance to this campaign—led by the famous Chiricahua leader, Geronimo—and the military's response to that resistance became known as the "Apache Campaign."

The Apache Campaign was sensationalized in the press, and inevitably, the Apache people were portrayed as "warlike" and "uncivilized." The negative images became commonplace, while the richness of the Apache culture became obscured and lost in a cloud of stereotypes.

In the Apachean Documentation Project at the New York museum, funded by the National Endowment for the Humanities, Cécile R. Ganteaume, an assistant curator, and Edgar Perry, director of the White Mountain Apache Cultural Center in Whiteriver, Ariz., are consolidating all ex-

isting documentation relating to NMAI's Apache collection in a computerized data base. The researchers also have brought Apache specialists to the museum to examine each object in order to improve its documentation. Project personnel identified methods of manufacture, materials, decoration techniques, activities in which the objects were used, and probable dates of object manufacture and/or use. Wherever possible, they also tried to identify the original Apache owners of the objects.

Many, if not most, of the Apache objects in the collection had never been exhibited, photographed or described in writing. The bulk of the collection had remained undisturbed in storage vaults since its accession by the museum in the early 1900s. "The lack of attention given to the Apache collection reflects a broader lack of attention given to the Apache culture throughout the scholarly community," Ganteaume says.

Researcher Bruce Smith is also involved in correcting misconceptions about American Indians. A member of the Department of Anthropology at the Natural History Museum, Smith has worked for more than a decade on a long-term research project demonstrating that the Indians of eastern North America were planting, harvesting, storing

(From left) Cécile Ganteaume of the Museum of the American Indian, intern Ellen Davis, Alan Ferg of the Arizona State Museum and White Mountain Apache Edgar Perry work with the Museum of the American Indian collections in a project to improve the documentation of the Apache objects. (Photo by Adams Taylor)

Wild Ozark gourds were discovered by archaeobiologists Bruce Smith and Wes Cowan in a Museum of Natural History project along the Buffalo River in Arkansas in 1990. Analysis of the seeds revealed that the gourds are the ancestors of modern summer squashes, adding another crop to the known indigenous plants domesticated by Native Americans in eastern North America about 4,000 years ago. (Photo by Wes Cowan)

and processing seeds from a variety of domesticated plants as early as 4,000 years ago.

"The textbooks say that maize and other domesticated plants came to the eastern woodlands from Mexico," Smith says. "They assume that the eastern [portion of what is now the] United States was a stagnant backwater and that the Indians here sat around passively, waiting for Mesoamerica to send them the gift of agriculture."

Evidence of this independently developed pre-maize agriculture can be seen in the many archaeological sites that have been excavated in the eastern United States in the last 10 years. These sites have been the focus of a level of archaeological activity unparalleled anywhere else in the world.

In earlier excavations, remains of seeds were seldom retrieved. "The seeds were simply too tiny and fragile," Smith says. "But in the late 1970s, a flotation technique was developed that easily separates seeds from soil samples.

"By the early 1980s," Smith continues, "I began to think that something was wrong with the long-held and current theory that agriculture had come to the East from Mesoamerica and that farming did not develop until after 800, when domesticated maize was introduced—so the story went—from Mexico.

"As I studied the problem, it became clear to me that this major cultural transformation—the transition from hunting and gathering to an agricultural economy—was longer and more gradual than generally believed.

"Even though these early farmers were not maize agriculturalists, they were farmers, and they behaved like farmers in obvious ways. They planted, harvested, stored and processed the seeds from a variety of cultivated and domesticated crops and, fortunately, left behind richly detailed evidence of these farming activities in the pits, middens and houses of their settlements."

To demonstrate that these early farmers were deliberately storing seeds for future planting, Smith began in 1982 to search for well-preserved, stored seeds from early farming settlements. And he found a key seed cache—in a Smithsonian collection storage area, a short walk from his office.

The cache was originally discovered by a Smithsonian archaeologist in 1956 in a charred grass basket at Russell Cave, Ala. Some of the seeds from this basket were dated at approximately A.D. 1. When subjected to scanning-electron-microscope analysis, they showed unequivocal evidence of domestication.

Seeking to learn more about the prehistoric potential of pre-maize seed plants, their habitats, present-day geographic range and harvest-yield potential, Smith embarked on a search for wild stands of goosefoot and sumpweed, two of the

Any man who has ever longed for fame might wish to have a daughter in the mold of Mary Anna Henry, who spent her spinsterhood as a champion of her father's place in history.

Her father was no less a figure than Joseph Henry, the first great American scientist after Benjamin Franklin. Henry was also the first secretary of the Smithsonian and the leading member of the American scientific community during most of the 19th century.

Working in the 1880s and 1890s, Mary Anna Henry gathered together many of her father's personal papers, scientific diaries and correspondence and set out to write his biography. This, she hoped, would establish once and for all that it was her father, not the British scientist Michael Faraday, who discovered the important principle of electromagnetic induction—the process of converting magnetism into electricity.

Mary Henry never completed her labor of love, but 100 years later, a small group of researchers at the Smithsonian continues her efforts to rescue Joseph Henry from relative obscurity.

The rescue is in the form of a comprehensive 15-volume project, *The Papers of Joseph Henry,* and in this effort, the historians are not relying on acts of filial devotion to tell Joseph Henry's story. Rather, under the direction of Marc Rothenberg, a historian of science and technology, the Smithsonian group has tracked down nearly 60,000 documents by Henry and his contemporaries.

Henry could well be considered an American success story. He was born into a poor family and, as he later said, was "principally self-educated." By the time he was 30, he had been an apprentice to a silversmith and a watchmaker, a schoolteacher, a chemical assistant, a surveyor on a state road project, and a professor of mathematics and natural philosophy at the Academy in his hometown of Albany, N.Y.

He then served for 14 years as an outstanding professor of physical science at

Joseph Henry and his family pause during a game of croquet on the National Mall around 1865. Henry's eldest daughter, Mary Anna (thought to be the person standing), labored many years to document Henry's accomplishments. The papers she gathered are now in the Smithsonian Archives.

the College of New Jersey (now Princeton University). And, in 1846, he moved to Washington, a village of marshland and mosquitoes, to direct the newly founded Smithsonian.

There, he spurred the development of many branches of science across the nation by enlisting the government's support of research. During his 31 years of leadership, the Smithsonian became a major basic research organization.

"Henry was above all an astute observer of his times," founding Henry Papers editor Nathan Reingold says. "The Joseph Henry papers re-create not only the great events and ideas of the times but also the subtle texture of the past."

To re-create the past so vividly requires diligent sleuthing and patience. Even with the Mary Henry heritage and a treasury of Henry-related papers in the Smithsonian Archives, it was clear that the collection did not document the full story of Henry's rich intellectual life. The search for additional

papers eventually led to a worldwide hunt, resulting in manuscripts from 17 countries and 300 institutions.

The papers demonstrate clearly Henry's belief in the importance of science and research. As he once told his colleagues after citing the many cases where seemingly pure science had benefited mankind, "These instances should teach us to dispise [sic] no persuit [sic] in science because its utility cannot be immediately perceived.... Most discoveries are unproductive until the progress of science in after years directs their application to purposes of practical utility."

As to Mary Henry's claim, Faraday was given credit for discovering electrical induction because he was the first to publish his results, but Henry's documents reveal that he had observed that phenomenon virtually simultaneously. Henry, it happens, admired Faraday greatly and visited him during a trip to Europe. ✴

plants cultivated by these prehistoric farmers. In two long autumn drives through the Midwest and Southeast, he located remnant stands of these plants in nine states, in both floodplain and upland locations, in agricultural fields, vacant lots and under bridges. He harvested the plants by hand, stripped them and, later, subjected them to laboratory analysis. In general, the harvest yield of these plants was high—especially the goosefoot. Smith believes that is why it was domesticated prehistorically.

The cabinets in Smith's office are filled with bottles and plastic trays containing the tens of thousands of seeds from these field studies. There and in the field he is hard at work "to pull together a number of different puzzle pieces to form the basis for an entirely new perspective on cultural evolution in prehistoric eastern North America."

A Sharper View of U.S. History

History is the yarn that weaves together the many experiences that have created the nation's social and cultural fabric. Often, however, our view of the past—our "shared humanity," as a recent report on history education put it—does not reflect the richness of the five-century-long metamorphosis triggered by European exploration of the New World. Nor does it pay heed to the antecedents, in the New World and the Old, of the world's greatest experiment in democracy. Our recollection of the past is more often an abbreviated ethnocentric linear procession of banner events, punctuated with the names of a few important individuals, rather than the wonderful tapestry that is our history.

In many Smithsonian bureaus and offices, scholars are devoted to synthesizing and integrating American history, sewing the seams that connect past to present and future. This research yields the balanced perspective that is history's most valuable contribution to society. As Alexis de Tocqueville, the 19th-century French author and statesman, warned, ignorance of history may make us prisoners of the past. Today, we might add that ignorance of our past leaves it hostage to the interpretations of others and us hostage to them.

The search for the broader meaning of the past has intensified in recent years. The "new social history" addresses the past not as isolated episodes occurring in a vacuum but as the product of prevailing societal conditions. Then as now, cause and effect—action and reaction, motive and consequence—is not a tidy progression. The true significance of historically important events can be appreciated only in the context of complex forces shaping society over time.

Historical Artifacts Unlock the Past

Perhaps the most difficult question put to historians is the one asked most often: "What was it like then?" Indeed, this question underlies much historical research today, and the search for historical context is bringing growing numbers of scholars to the Smithsonian's museums and archives. As keeper of many historically important records and key elements of the nation's material heritage, the Institution holds keys that can help to unlock our past.

In recent years, the artifacts in the Smithsonian's collections have grown in importance as tools for scholarship. In some cases, the trappings of bygone eras—clothing, furniture, toys, clocks, machinery, pottery, coins and medical equipment, to name a few—supplement findings from written documents, the mainstays of historical research. Increasingly, however, material artifacts open entirely new areas of inquiry, permitting historians, anthropologists, folklorists and others to pose questions that cannot be answered through traditional research channels. What better way to study the attitudes and lifestyles of a particular era or to trace the evolution of a field of technology than with objects from that era?

In a study conducted at the National Air and Space Museum, for example, engineers performed a technical analysis of the Wright Flyer. The review of the world's first airplane yielded new insights into how the Wright brothers overcame the technical obstacles confronting them and others who raced to accomplish the first in powered flight. Continuing this line of investigation, historian Peter Jakab has written a book on the inventive process that led to the successful Wright Flyer.

And at the National Museum of American History, curator Richard Ahlborn and Russian American scholars from several institutions re-examined the 350 Old Russian "traveling" icons and crosses purchased by George Brown Goode, assistant secretary in charge of the U.S. National Museum, before the turn of the century. Research on the cast-copper devotional objects—some dating back to 1650—revealed much about the practices and beliefs of the 1,000-year-old Russian Orthodox Church, especially those of a sect known as the Old Believers, which split from the main church in 1667. In 1988, on the millennium of the advent of Christianity among Slavs, the museum presented an exhibit of the icons and a daylong symposium with illustrated lectures and choral music. In a recent publication on the results of detailed technical and historical analyses, researchers describe how copper-alloy castings were made and trace the evolution of design and customs over time and across geographic clusters of church members. Such studies encourage investigations into the past and present traditions of the Russian Orthodox Church, including communities of Old Believers in the United States.

Collections-related research not only illuminates previously unlit areas of history but also enables scholars to penetrate the crust of common perceptions. For example, a new look at how government photographers portrayed American life during the 1930s departed from traditional perceptions of these New Deal depictions. Combing the files of the National Archives and the Library of Congress, researchers from the National Museum of American Art and the Museum of American History reviewed not only the pictures commissioned by the Farm Security Agency, whose photographers produced the most searing and most famous images of the Great Depression, but also those taken for other government agencies. The contrasts were often striking, revealing much about the agencies and their agendas. Often, the agencies used the photographs to promote their particular missions, as well as to reinforce the institutionalized racial and sex biases operating at the time.

Of course, many important elements of the past cannot be preserved as material artifacts. The Smithsonian is also dedicated to preserving the ephemeral, yet quintessential, aspects of American society—the nation's rich musical, dramatic and oral heritage. The Anacostia Museum, which is devoted to African American history, culture and art, and the Museum of American History recapture these elusive elements of the past through interpretive programs based on scholarly research of oral traditions and popular culture. Smithsonian Folkways Records documents and disseminates worldwide musical, narrative and spoken-word traditions. The Festival of American Folklife, produced by the Smithsonian's Center for Folklife Program and Cultural Studies, has exposed millions of people to the cultural traditions of various ethnic and regional groups.

Dedication to authenticity characterizes all of these efforts, which benefit from the extensive holdings of the Smithsonian's various archives. For example, a celebration of the 90th anniversary of the birth of Duke Ellington was guided by studies of the Smithsonian's huge collection of the composer/band leader's scores, tapes and memorabilia. Many of the more than 2,000 musical instruments in the collections of the American History Museum are still used to create beautiful sounds. The Smithsonian has a group of resident musicians who make up the core of four renowned performing ensembles. One, the Smithson String Quartet, performs a classical and early romantic quartet repertoire on period instruments. The authentic performance programs of the string quartet, the Smithsonian Chamber Players and the Smithsonian Chamber Orchestra marry the original instruments with the music composed for them. A recent addition to the Smithsonian's Chamber Music Program is the Castle Trio, whose repertoire of pieces played on period instruments includes works from the late 18th through the 19th centuries.

And, not least, the Smithsonian has undertaken a major expansion of its jazz programs, including establishment of a resident jazz orchestra to perform a repertoire based on accurate transcriptions and original manuscripts of the classic

Remember the "silent majority," the purportedly large segment of the population that many politicians claimed to represent during the 1970s? How about the "smilin' majority"? Chances are you never encountered that play on words. But you would have, were it not for an 11th-hour decision by Pepsi Cola and its advertising agency to shelve a sales campaign pitched to the "smilin' majority." Instead of mixing politics and soft drinks, the agency and the company chose to continue on the advertising path blazed by the successful "Pepsi generation," a phrase permanently ingrained in the minds of many Americans.

The Pepsi campaign is just one highlight among many episodes in the history of American advertising. Mirroring life in the United States in instructive and intriguing ways, this history is the subject of major research and collecting programs in the National Museum of American History's Archives Center, an eclectic repository of manuscripts, ephemera and other historical documents.

The archives' advertising history collections, along with the Center for Advertising History, are the nation's primary resources for studying American society as portrayed by the advertising industry. Through its growing collection of print, audio and video materials, the archives opens a window to that vision of life reproduced in the commercial imagery of advertising agencies and their clients. These images convey information about social values, practices and stereotypes, as well as consumer behavior and patterns of work and recreation. They also chronicle the evolution of advertising design and of national and international marketing techniques.

Staff members of the Center for Advertising History, which concentrates on the development of advertising since World War II, are conducting comprehensive case studies of successful advertising campaigns. They collect scripts, storyboards, audio- and videotapes, research reports, sales figures and other key items, and they conduct oral-history interviews with pivotal figures in the campaigns.

A primary goal of these efforts is to support research on the nation's economic, cultural and social history. Historians, journalists, designers, marketing specialists and congressional aides are among the researchers who consult the unique collection of advertising materials.　✳

Way above all other Flour.

This 1890s advertisement for Washburn Crosby flour, part of the Museum of American History's Warshaw Collection of Business Americana, provides a look into advertising history. The study of advertising also reveals changing styles in society, gender roles and costume.

works of Ellington and other jazz greats. The initiative also involves launching Jazz Masterworks editions of publications of classic works for the jazz orchestra. A grant of $7 million from the Lila Wallace-Readers Digest Fund is making possible a 10-year partnership, "America's Jazz Heritage," involving traveling exhibitions, radio programs, educational materials and more.

Everyday Life in America

As we go through our daily paces, change is almost indiscernible, masked by the deceptive routines of everyday life. But look back. The oldest among us have witnessed the triumph of manned flight, two world wars and conflicts in Korea and Vietnam, the birth of the nuclear bomb, the Great Depression, the growth of suburbs and the demise of many a central city, the civil rights movement, the energy crisis, the victory over polio, the emergence of AIDS, the "harnessing" of the atom, the computer revolution and the exploration of space. As the maxim has it, the only constant is change.

And yet, another adage also holds true: The more things change, the more they remain the same. Baseball remains the national pastime; most American adults are intent on owning their own homes; and advertisers continue to beckon us to spend our dollars on their products (see "Of Hype and History," Page 82).

Much of the historical research under way at the Smithsonian takes an integrated view of the past, explaining how important episodes influence and are influenced by society. Though historic events are often associated with the deeds of famous Americans, the true significance of many of these events can be appreciated only when their impact on ordinary citizens is understood.

Emblematic of this approach is the series of American History Museum exhibitions on the evolution of everyday life in America since the 17th century. Curators are working on the last two exhibitions in this series. These exhibitions, developed by the Department of Social and Cultural History, will focus on life in the 19th and 20th centuries. An exhibition on the impact of science on American life, based on research in the Department of the History of Science and Technology, is due to open in 1994. That exhibition will permit visitors to explore the evolution of the scientific enterprise and how, as a major force of change in this century, science has transformed society and individual lives. The exhibition on life since 1900 will explore other agents of change as well—possible subjects for inclusion are World War II, the civil

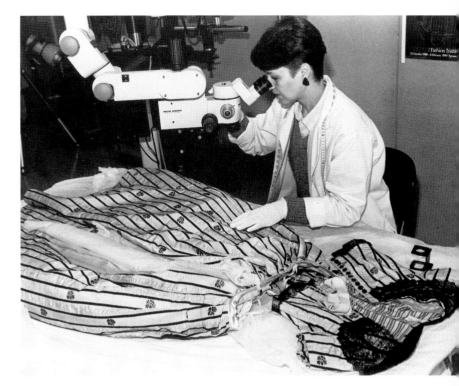

rights movement, mass communications, the transformation from a manufacturing economy to one based on services, the growth of suburban communities. From these vantage points, visitors will be able to assess how Americans have accommodated to and resisted change and how they have sought to influence the forces shaping their lives.

Barometers of Social Change

The Smithsonian's collections offer many windows on the past and the present. Artifacts of one age can be compared with counterparts in another. Changes from one era to the next are likely to reflect much more than growing technological sophistication, although that, too, is important.

An especially rich source of information on people's lives and attitudes and on social mores is the American History Museum's large collection of period clothing, fashion accessories, grooming items and related artifacts. Past studies of how people dressed—or, more precisely, the image they sought to convey through dress—revealed much about class distinctions, lifestyles and stereotypes. In turn, changes in dress have not only symbolized, but sometimes catalyzed, social change.

In a study now considered a classic in the field of social history, curator Claudia Kidwell of the Division of Costume and her associate, Margaret Christman, described how the rise of the ready-to-wear clothing industry during the late 1800s and

Conservator Polly Willman examines the weave of a stunning silk brocade dress that belonged to first lady Mary Todd Lincoln. By studying how patterning is achieved in the fabric, Willman was able to decide how best to preserve the gown for "First Ladies: Political Role and Public Image," an exhibition at the Museum of American History that re-interprets the role of the nation's first ladies in light of new research. (Photo by Doc Dougherty)

the 1900s produced important forces of equality in the United States. The study resulted in a book and in a museum exhibition. Both illustrated that the industry's evolution, propelled by advances in mass-production technology, brought fashion to nearly all Americans. People began to dress alike, and clothing was no longer an unmistakable badge of the wearer's social status and occupation. Of course, this story has many elements, some of them unsavory, such as the brutal sweatshop conditions in clothing factories and home workshops.

As a result of the clothing revolution, Americans attained a reputation as the best-dressed people in the world, with at least the appearance of equality. Even Soviet leader Nikita Khrushchev noticed. In recalling his 1959 meeting with New York's Gov. Nelson Rockefeller, Khrushchev said that, as one of the nation's richest men, Rockefeller "certainly wasn't dressed in cheap clothes, but I wouldn't say he was dressed elegantly either. He was dressed more or less like other Americans."

As a counterpoint to the Soviet leader's comments, Kidwell and Christman cite social critic Michael Harrington's observation that "it is much easier in the United States to be decently dressed than it is to be decently housed, fed or doctored."

In a more recent book, *Men and Women: Dressing the Part,* Kidwell and collaborators from other institutions examined the evolution of gender identity and gender roles as reflected in clothing and hair-style changes. A recent exhibition, "Men and Women: A History of Costume, Gender and Power," organized in collaboration with museum social historian Barbara Clark Smith, also explored these themes.

Studies of the past also reveal striking parallels with the present. Though the particulars of each era usually differ in important ways, comparisons can enlighten, revealing universal concerns and providing benchmarks for gauging social progress. Consider the antecedent of today's women's movement. During the Progressive Era (1890–1925), women organized into a potent political force, fighting for many causes with parallels in the agendas of today's women's organizations.

At that time, however, mainstream grass-roots women's movements did not directly challenge male-dominated spheres of activity. Instead, women acted indirectly by expanding their own sphere of activity, often centered on the home. "'We don't want to enter a man's world; we just want to carry out women's roles effectively.' That

was the message," says Edith Mayo, curator in the Division of Political History at the American History Museum. Mayo's studies of the rhetoric and images of the era reveal that women's groups used the "sanctity of the home" as a rallying point for efforts to protect the moral and physical welfare of the family from corrupt officialdom.

By 1915, the Woman's Christian Temperance Union, suffrage societies and women's club movement together counted some 5 million members. The organizations served as alternative political parties. The exhibition developed by Mayo, "From Parlor to Politics: Women and Reform in America, 1890–1925," explores how the influential women's network succeeded in securing child-labor reforms, as well as the passage of important public-health and environmental laws. The groups virtually created the consumer movement, and they triumphed in their efforts to make kindergartens part of public school systems. Women's organizations also actively supported the League of Nations and the international peace movement following World War I. Two constitutional amendments—women's suffrage and prohibition—are legacies of the Progressive Era women's movement.

Other examples of continuity and change in American society come from the arena of political campaigning. Voters and political observers today bemoan tactics that place style over substance and appearance over qualifications. They usually allot the most blame for this situation to the role of television. Since 1789, however, American political campaigns have been filled with image consciousness and personal attacks. The American History Museum's collection of more than 40,000 campaign objects—buttons, badges, papers, jewelry, hats, toys and other items—bears out this truth.

Research by the museum's political historians traces the development of modern presidential campaigning, a feature of a book, *Hail to the Candidate.* Keith Melder, the curator who led the review of the campaign collections, pegs the birth of modern electioneering to Andrew Jackson, who organized a national popular campaign to avenge his 1824 defeat to John Quincy Adams. Almost immediately after his loss, "Old Hickory" began his run for the next national contest—the first four-year campaign. In the aftermath of his 1828 victory, two major political parties emerged and have dominated American elections for a century and a half.

Imagery and widespread popular participation were prominent features of American politics through the 19th century. In more recent years, the mass media have become the favored means of portraying candidates' images.

Television's central role in modern campaigns is studied at the museum by political historian William Bird Jr., who collects and analyzes political commercials. From the outset of televised political campaigns in the early 1950s, critics have complained that candidates are sold "like soap." Bird's aim is to document the lessons that advertisers and political publicists have taught each other since the 1930s.

Land of Diversity

The United States is known worldwide as a land of great cultural diversity, a nation built by immigrants. But our collective memory of the experiences of some ethnic and racial groups and the roles these groups have played in building American society has significant lapses. Until recently, the histories and cultural underpinnings of African Americans, Hispanic Americans, Asian Americans and Native Americans were badly neglected. As a result, there is a backlog of information to gather and study about these groups, which will in turn enhance understanding of our society as a whole.

In 1967, the Smithsonian sought to address this

Curator Spencer Crew of the Museum of American History carries out research on historic documents and memorabilia in preparing a traveling exhibition on black land grant colleges in America. (Photo by Eric Long)

"Climbing Jacob's Ladder: The Rise of Black Churches in Eastern American Cities, 1740–1877" attracted author Alex Haley to speak for the Smithsonian's Anacostia Museum in a televised public service announcement. (Photo by Dane Penland)

weakness in part by creating the Anacostia Museum, devoted to studying African American heritage and explaining the social, political and cultural contributions of African Americans. The museum's quest "is to see what and who preceded us," its founder and first director, the late John Kinard, wrote, "and, if we can, to understand how we survived. We want to look back over the roads we have trod and, in so doing, have the wisdom and tenacity to go forward with increased sensitivity and inspiration." In carrying out this mission, the museum, located in Southeast Washington, D.C., has drawn international recognition and inspired the creation of more than 100

museums devoted to African American history.

The Smithsonian has also set about indexing artifacts in the national collections according to ethnic association. The Afro-American Index Project is inventorying the vast collections of the American History Museum, the Natural History Museum, the Air and Space Museum, the Museum of American Art, the Hirshhorn Museum and Sculpture Garden, the National Portrait Gallery, the Smithsonian Archives and other bureaus, such as the Anacostia Museum itself. Together, the items in each bureau's collections will provide a broad foundation for studying the history and material culture of black Americans. The American History Museum is also indexing and preparing guides to Hispanic and Judaic ethnographic artifacts. Its novel Afro-American Community Project is gathering historical data on pre-Civil War communities of free blacks who lived in some Northern cities (see "Free Blacks Before the Civil War," below).

Scholars who concentrate on the role of ethnic groups in American history, a neglected part of the nation's past, often find that essential clues are widely scattered. For research on African Americans, fertile sources of information have been historically black colleges and universities, black churches and U.S. Census figures. But perhaps the richest source of all is African American individuals and families. Elderly African Americans, in particular, are the threads that link past to present. Smithsonian researchers rely heavily on personal interviews, plus the handful of African American oral-history projects under way at other institutions around the country.

Researchers fear, however, that many people with important stories to tell will die before sharing their knowledge. Their personal collections—papers, pictures, arts and crafts, and other artifacts—may be dispersed or even destroyed. To prevent this loss, the Anacostia Museum has encouraged local historical preservation efforts. The museum's Research Department organized the Anacostia Historical Society. A major exhibition, "The Anacostia Story: 1608–1930," recounting the history of one of the nation's oldest African American communities, was mounted. A new organization begun by the museum, the Friends for the Preservation of Afro-American Culture, is being schooled in the techniques of historical preservation, including genealogy, oral-history interviewing and exhibit methods.

In his study of the early history of black churches in the cities of the Eastern seaboard, former Anacostia Museum historian Edward D. Smith discovered that few church documents and artifacts from the period between 1740 and 1877 have survived. Much of Smith's success in documenting the rise of organized black churches—the spiritual, social, political, educational and cultural centers of African American communities—stemmed from

FREE BLACKS BEFORE THE CIVIL WAR

By the beginning of the 19th century, slavery was being abolished in the Northern states. After surviving perilous passage on the "underground railroad," black slaves were delivered to freedom in the North. In history books, the pre-Civil War story of African Americans who slipped from bondage in the South stops there. But what kind of life did the freed slaves find in the North? How did they fit into existing communities of free blacks, and what kinds of jobs did they find?

Historians have only begun to study free black communities of the antebellum period. Since 1981, the Afro-American Communities Project, housed in the American History Museum, has been systematically gathering the information necessary to fill this gap in historical understanding. Project staff, directed by James Horton, curator at the American History Museum and professor of American history and civilization at George Washington University, are analyzing the social, political and economic structure of Northern free black communities, from the Revolutionary War to the Civil War. The project is funded by the Smithsonian, the Ford Foundation, George Washington University and the National Endowment for the Humanities.

The researchers have compiled the most extensive data base on these communities ever assembled. Gathering information from censuses and other sources, the project has developed profiles of free black communities in Boston; Cincinnati; Philadelphia; Chicago; Buffalo; Detroit; San Francisco; and Oberlin, Ohio. Staff members are also assembling a data base from Veterans Administration files that contain information on the more than 2,000 black soldiers who served in the Union army. A third data base under development uses information culled from 19th-century newspapers, personal papers and organizational records, describing more than 300 black abolitionist leaders.

To enrich these resources, Horton and his associates are scrutinizing supplemental sources. A pilot study in Boston draws on probate court records. This information will also be collected in other communities, permitting historians to address important questions related to the occupational and social status of free blacks.

The project's work has already yielded important insights. Comparisons between cities reveal that the familial, organizational and political structure of free black communities was extremely complex, a fact not apparent when only single communities are studied. ✳

A young Zuni Pueblo woman performs a ceremony with the "olla," or water jar, at a Festival of American Folklife event. (Photo by Howard Barbie)

finding elderly people who had safeguarded the histories of their congregations. Smith's comprehensive search, resulting in the book and exhibition "Climbing Jacob's Ladder: The Rise of Black Churches in Eastern American Cities, 1740–1877," took him to churches, libraries, seminaries, historical societies, museums and homes all along the East Coast. Smith showed how the first "visible" black churches provided educational opportunities, nurtured economic development and produced generations of strong leaders.

For Spencer Crew, then curator in the Department of Social and Cultural History at the American History Museum, three years of preliminary work were necessary to ferret out details of the 1915-to-1940 mass exodus of African Americans from the rural South to the urban North. More than 1 million Southern blacks participated in this search for economic opportunity in the factories of the industrialized North. Although this Great Migration profoundly changed American society and the lives of its participants, it had not attracted the scholarly attention it deserved.

Crew employed innovative research methods that went beyond scrutinizing newspaper articles from the period and reviewing the records and oral histories gathered by various centers interested in African American history. For one, he attended reunions of families whose members took part in the Great Migration, to gather accounts of actual participants and their descendants. This information gave Crew insight into the uncertainties and complex choices people faced as they weighed the decision to move. With this information, he developed a fuller and clearer picture of the discrimination and abysmal living conditions that drove many African Americans from the South. And he learned what it was like to move into a new environment where reality often did not match expectations or aspirations. African Americans who moved North, Crew concluded, "were just as heroic as Western pioneers, who also desired a better life."

The product of Crew's research, the exhibition "Field to Factory: Afro-American Migration, 1915–1940," is on display at the American History Museum, and a version of the exhibition is now traveling to museums across the country.

Preserving Living Traditions

To understand a culture—whether defined by ethnic origin, place of settlement or occupation—requires appreciation of a people's customs, arts, crafts, songs and stories. Taken together, these folk customs express forms of knowledge, wisdom and aesthetics derived from centuries of creativity. If cultural traditions wither, people in that group lose a major source of their uniqueness and pride; if cultures die, the human cultural repertoire is diminished.

Countering the homogenizing forces of mass culture, the Smithsonian's Center for Folklife Programs and Cultural Studies seeks to preserve the many expressions of cultural diversity that enrich American society. Through its international programs, the Center describes and conserves the follife traditions of people in other nations (see "International Commitment to Cultural Diversity," Page 90). Each domestic and international project is characterized by a unique blend of research, education and cultural preservation.

The most visible product of this mission is the Smithsonian's Festival of American Folklife. Since 1967, millions of visitors have come to the National Mall in Washington, D.C., for this outdoor celebration of cultural diversity. Collectively, the festivals have presented more than 14,000 traditional musicians, craftspeople and other artists from more than 45 countries, every region in the United States, more than 100 American Indian tribes and scores of ethnic communities. Visitors have observed, enjoyed and learned about unique traditions, directly experiencing the benefits of preserving cultural heritage. In turn, international recognition of the participating artists and artisans enhances their commitment to practicing and teaching their unique skills and to passing on the lore of their individual cultures.

The Folklife Festival has served as the inspiration behind two other national programs devoted to the preservation of folk traditions: the American Folklife Center at the Library of Congress and the National Endowment for the Arts Program in the Folk Arts. States and communities have also responded by creating their own local means of preserving traditions.

The Festival, like the Center for Folklife Programs' films, videotapes, books, recordings and other educational tools, is the product of a far-flung research program to document, interpret and present folklife traditions. The studies of staff folklorists, cultural anthropologists and ethnomusicologists are supplemented by the contributions of outside researchers. In any given year, about 200 such projects are under way.

Folkways Records, administered by the Folklife Programs Center, became part of the Smithsonian in 1987. Founded in 1947 by the dedicated Moses Asch, Folkways built up a catalog of more than 2,200 published albums of tremendous diversity — music, from early classical to electronic; documented recordings of more than 700 native peoples of the world; instrument and language instruction records; readings from ancient and modern literature, in English and other languages; songs and games for children in several languages; and a science series, including sounds of North American frogs and an introduction to human biology. Folkways also offers a collection of historical and documentary readings of the words of historical figures, such as Theodore Roosevelt, Booker T.

Washington, John F. Kennedy, Franklin and Eleanor Roosevelt, Martin Luther King Jr., Joseph McCarthy and Carl Sandburg, to name but a few.

The Center, says director Richard Kurin, is infused by the belief that "cultural pluralism is a national strength." Its programs blend traditional ethnographic research — systematic documentation and interpretation of the heritage of communities — with cultural advocacy. Rather than working only to salvage specimens of fading traditions, the Center's researchers use their findings to help perpetuate the folkways of individual cultures. After the music and other traditions of Louisiana's Cajun community were showcased in several of the early festivals, for example, the state experienced a Cajun revival. Its pride rejuvenated, the community invested greater effort in preserving its identity, and public agencies contributed to measures to ensure the continued existence of this cultural treasure.

Bill Birchfield, from Tennessee, plays old-time country music during a 1986 Festival of American Folklife performance. (Photo by Laurie Minor-Penland)

In Delhi, during the mid-1970s, bulldozers leveled a slum that provided housing to several hundred folk artists. And under the guise of a poverty eradication program, some of these itinerant musicians, craftspeople, puppeteers, acrobats and other performers were forcibly sterilized. Defined as beggars, those artisans who continued to practice their traditions were harassed by law-enforcement officials.

Today, however, India celebrates its folk traditions in government-sponsored regional centers for the study and presentation of folk culture; the government has also funded crafts training and marketing programs. Efforts to establish a permanent settlement for the Delhi folk artists are under way, and the government initiated a national cultural festival.

This striking reversal is the product of many efforts, including those of the Smithsonian's Office of Folklife Programs, now the Center for Folklife Programs and Cultural Studies. In 1985, following a period of intensive research, the office mounted two major living demonstrations of Indian folk traditions and prepared ethnographic films, catalogs and an array of other supplementary education materials. Together with the Natural History Museum, and with the intensive collaboration of Indian designers, scholars and community developers, the office developed the exhibition "Aditi: A Celebration of Life," which featured thousands of traditional objects and 40 Indian folk artists. "Mela! An Indian Fair," a re-creation of an Indian festival with some 60 performers and artists, was part of the Festival of American Folklife.

The exhibitions, attracting nearly 2 million visitors, were acclaimed in the United States and around the world. Impressed by the overwhelming response, then Prime Minister Rajiv Gandhi hailed the participating folk artists as his country's foremost cultural ambassadors. This recognition triggered developments in India that now help safeguard and promote the country's folk traditions and their practitioners.

Though this may be the most dramatic result of its international programs of cultural research, education and conservation, the Center for Folklife Programs is making contributions across the world. Since 1967, Folklife Programs has collaborated with scholars and organizations in nearly 50 countries, from Senegal to Vietnam. ✳

Ten-year-old Bundu Khan Langa demonstrates Rajasthani musical traditions for visitors to the 1985 exhibition "Aditi: A Celebration of Life" in the Museum of Natural History. Research for the exhibition examined how styles and skills in India are passed from one generation to the next. (Photo by Chip Clark)

Placing Science and Technology in Context

The milestones marking a nation's progress are often its scientific and technological achievements. Traditionally, historical investigations of these accomplishments have focused on the process of discovery and invention and on the individuals involved. Until recently, far less attention has been paid to the social impacts of these achievements.

The Smithsonian's Air and Space Museum and Museum of American History are at the forefront of a movement to address the social dynamics of scientific and technological change and to describe and explain its broader historical context. New and planned exhibitions, focusing on science and technology and examining their effects on society, will contribute to the scientific literacy of the American public (see "The Information Age: People, Information & Technology," Page 92). This approach recognizes science and technology as a major social force that produces benefits, imposes costs and sometimes introduces new risks and uncertainties.

Technological Progress: Gains and Losses

In 1753, the owner of a New Jersey copper mine imported an English-built steam engine to pump water from the mine's shafts. The imported technology was more costly than it was effective. One of the first attempts to transfer technology from a developed country to an undeveloped land was a failure. Nearly four decades later, again in New Jersey, a partnership of private entrepreneurs and the state and federal governments launched a program to encourage the start-up of manufacturing businesses in the city of Paterson. The experiment floundered, the victim of local opposition, bad management and other problems.

These episodes, two of many studied by Smithsonian historians in their research on the American Industrial Revolution, are strikingly similar to some modern endeavors. Today, of course, the United States is on the exporting end of technology transfers, but the process is still fraught with difficulty.

This 1890s photograph of the National Cash Register machine shop in Dayton, Ohio, yields dramatic evidence of the changes in the workplace brought about by the Industrial Revolution. These changes are documented by researchers in the Museum of American History.

"THE INFORMATION AGE: PEOPLE, INFORMATION & TECHNOLOGY"

By now, most everyone knows that we are living in the midst of the "computer revolution," an age of "electronic information." Although still the same physical size, the world has become perceptibly smaller—a "global village" linked by instantaneous communications.

More so than any other sweeping development, the rise of the ubiquitous semiconductor chip and other electrical information devices inspired an array of phrases that attempt to capture the enormous changes wrought by technology. Yet, all failed to convey the depth and breadth of this rapid social transformation, perhaps because scholar and layman alike had yet to reckon with its full dimensions.

This is precisely what an interdisciplinary team of researchers at the American History Museum and their colleagues from other institutions has accomplished. In developing one of the most ambitious exhibitions ever undertaken by the Smithsonian, the researchers mounted the first comprehensive effort to interpret the many ways in which information technology has influenced virtually every aspect of our lives.

Thus, research for the exhibition hall, "Information Age: People, Information & Technology," touches on important issues—such as those related to the protection of privacy—and historical themes that, to date, have received scant attention from social historians. "Most research has focused on the development of the technology itself," David Allison, the exhibition's chief historian, explains. "The incredible story of chip making and miniaturization is important, and we tell it in the exhibition. But our emphasis is on the social applications and implications of the technology. We want to show what history can tell us about today's developments."

History does contain events and experiences that parallel those in our "high-tech" era. Consider the milestone hailed as a "wondrous event of a wondrous age," the laying of the first trans-Atlantic cable, completed on Sept. 1, 1858. This link making telegraphic communication possible between England and the United States was trumpeted in newspaper headlines throughout the country. The euphoria stemmed not only from national pride over a major technological feat, but also from the expectations that the communication link engendered. Then, as now, information was recognized as a source of power, and some in the United States viewed the trans-Atlantic cable as a route for spreading the American form of democracy.

The exhibition traces the roots of the current Information Age to Samuel Morse's invention of the telegraph, the first means of instantaneous communication. Visitors examine the succeeding advances in information technologies—telephones, radios, early business processing equipment, military code-breaking equipment and the first computer—that led to the current profusion of electronic information devices. Throughout, the social consequences of each advance are outlined.

To develop the exhibition, museum researchers consulted closely with computer and communications firms, many of which also donated funds and equipment to the exhibition. These donations allowed Smithsonian staff to make the exhibition one of the most highly interactive galleries ever done, pioneering many new multimedia displays. ✳

ENIAC, an 18,000-vacuum-tube electronic computer, marked the beginning, in 1946, of large-scale digital electronic computation. A small portion of ENIAC is exhibited in the Museum of American History's "Information Age" exhibition.

"Engines of Change," an American History Museum exhibition organized by Steven Lubar, a curator in the Division of Engineering and Industry, and Brooke Hindle, former senior historian at the museum, offers many interesting comparisons and contrasts between today and the era between the late 1700s and 1860 that marked the U.S. ascent to industrial greatness. Though the differences are considerable, the two periods are notable for their similar effects on workers. The rapid development of manufacturing in the Industrial Revolution marked a transformation in the lives of workers, who exchanged the autonomy of agrarian and artisan occupations for the regimentation and regular wages of factory work. Today, the growth of foreign competition, the drive to automate and the transition to a service economy are eliminating traditional jobs, and the employment alternatives often do not match workers' skills and aspirations.

Agricultural Mechanization

American farmers are the most productive in the world, a status attributed to the superiority of the nation's agricultural technology. Farmers represent less than 5 percent of the U.S. population, but they produce more than enough food to feed the nation. At the turn of the century, however, when agriculture was a labor-intensive enterprise, more than half the population lived on farms.

Behind these statistics lies a story of tremendous change, driven by mechanization, government policies, two world wars and many other factors. To historian Pete Daniel of the American History Museum, this 20th-century transformation represents one of the best examples of the relationship between technology and societal changes. Focusing on the South, Daniel is exploring the demise of the Jeffersonian ideal—family-owned small farms—and the consequences of the "mechanical enclosure movement," which concentrated agricultural production among large farming operations.

"I end up raising more questions than I answer," says Daniel, who has evaluated in two recent books how life in the rural South was changed by the substitution of machines and capital for agricultural labor. Though controversial, the books have generated discussion on an essential question: Was the price of mechanization worth the gains? Historians have yet to answer this question satisfactorily, Daniel says.

Hardly a romantic about the rural South of the early 1900s, Daniel has documented racial discrimination, as well as the dismal living conditions of many African American and white tenant farm-

ers and sharecroppers. But he also has examined some of the social costs of displacing thousands of agricultural workers with machinery. Many workers had no option but to abandon their rural communities to move to cities in the North and South.

Daniel and his colleagues approach the complex 20th-century history of the rural South from many angles. In an oral-history project, fellow researcher Lou Ann Jones has interviewed nearly 200 rural Southerners who lived through the changes wrought by science, technology, government policies, population movements and evolving race relations. Excerpts of these life stories—prepared from nearly 40,000 pages of interview transcripts—will be published in a forthcoming book.

Another major focus of research is the period between 1940 and the early 1960s. Sandwiched between the New Deal and the civil rights eras, this two-decade span was also marked by important changes that have influenced the life and culture of the South. Indeed, many historians now believe that the roots of the Southern civil rights movement can be traced directly to tensions generated when millions of African Americans left the rural South and competed for jobs in the North during World War II.

A proposed agricultural hall will reflect the results of these and other studies. Museum visitors will be able to weigh the costs and benefits of agricultural mechanization and the rise of manufacturing, confronting the same critical questions that have motivated the historian's research.

Larry Jones (right), with the Museum of American History's Division of Conservation, and representatives of Lummus Industries supervise the removal of a cotton gin from a shed near Macon, Ga., in March 1990. The gin, restored by Lummus, the original manufacturer, is now on view in the museum, helping to illustrate the story of cotton cultivation in the South. (Photo by Richard Hofmeister)

Air and Space History

Curator for Soviet space programs Cathleen Lewis stands in front of an engineering model of the Soviet Vega spacecraft that traveled to the planet Venus and to Comet Halley. The Air and Space Museum is extracting details from objects to study the Soviet space program. (Photo by Rick Vargas)

The National Air and Space Museum, founded in 1946, has become one of the world's most popular museums since moving into its new building in 1976. Its appeal for the approximately 8 million people who flock there each year stems from the museum's unparalleled collection of more than 250 historically significant aircraft and other items related to aerospace history, including satellites, rockets, guided missiles and spacecraft. These collections—more than 33,000 artifacts in all—not only illustrate the compelling stories of human flight and space exploration, but they also support an expanding and nationally important research program. Today, the museum is one of the premier centers for studying the history of air and space technology. It also supports the Center for Earth and Planetary Studies and an astrophysical laboratory focusing on infrared astronomy.

Aerospace history, though typically described in terms of science and engineering accomplishments, is primarily a story of human actions and impacts. Consider the tremendous growth in commercial air transportation and its impact on societies, a direct legacy of the Wright brothers. And in the three decades since Sputnik, space exploration has become an international race to exploit the extraterrestrial environment for a variety of purposes, including manufacturing and defense.

Building on its excellence in studies of the technical aspects of air and space flight, the museum has expanded its research to encompass the human elements of this technology. Moreover, the museum's researchers examine developments in air and space technology in the context of broader scientific and technological pursuits—nationally and internationally—and from the perspective of government policies.

Recent projects in the Department of Aeronautics illustrate this broad spectrum of interests. Curator of Air Transport R. E. G. Davies, for instance, has in the past published several comprehensive works on the history of the airline industry worldwide, with specialized volumes on the United States and Latin America, and he is currently working on *Airlines of Asia Since 1921.* More recently, he has embarked on a series of books under the general title of *Great Airlines of the World.* Already completed are the histories of Pan American, Lufthansa and Delta Air Lines, and one on the former Soviet Union's Aeroflot, largest airline in the world, is in preparation. This latter series is copiously illustrated in full color with maps, photographs and superb drawings by famous aviation artist Mike Machat.

Lasting contributions to aviation—and society in general—were also made by pioneering women and African American aviators. Their experiences, too, have been recorded by the museum's historians. In the exhibition and book "Black Wings: The American Black in Aviation," historians Von Hardesty and Dominick Pisano described how a consuming desire to fly ultimately enabled a handful of African Americans to achieve their dream in a segregated society—even if it meant going abroad. Inspired by Charles Lindbergh's trans-Atlantic flight in 1927, black Americans set out "to fill the air with black wings," pioneer black aviator William Powell wrote in *Black Wings,* published in 1934. This enthusiasm led to all-black flying clubs and air shows, which steadily increased the number of African American pilots—from fewer than 10 in 1930 to more than 100 in 1941.

During World War II, the all-black 332nd Fighter Group (the Tuskegee Airmen) made a significant

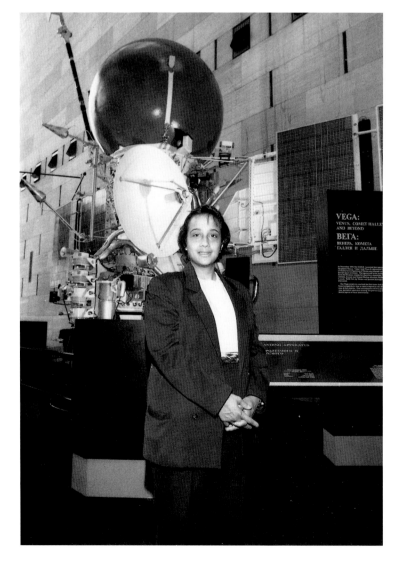

THE SMITHSONIAN INSTITUTION: A WORLD OF DISCOVERY

The unparalleled collections of the Air and Space Museum, including the Wright Flyer (center), the Spirit of St. Louis (upper right) and the Gemini 4 spacecraft (left), shown here in the Milestones of Flight Hall, make the museum one of the premier centers for studying the history of air and space technology. (Photo by Charles Phillips)

contribution to the war effort, paving the way for African Americans to play an increasing role in aerospace activities in the postwar decades. The museum continues to foster research on African Americans in aviation. Another Institution effort in this area was the 1991 Smithsonian Institution Press publication of *Benjamin O. Davis Jr.: American,* the autobiography of the first African American general in the U.S. Air Force, who was for a time commander of the Tuskegee Airmen. Davis has also been a very active adviser to the museum staff.

Women were quick to overcome the obstacles that kept them grounded. The first women to venture into the male domain of flying were viewed as oddities, according to a series published by museum historians. Newspapers dubbed the first women airplane passengers "superwomen."

Women aviators, though not common, were highly visible by the time the nation entered World War I. Their exploits were often chronicled by a captivated press. Women pilots lobbied hard for legislation that would allow them to serve as combat flyers during World War I, garnering the support of many congressmen but failing to sway the secretary of war. After the war, however, the ranks of women pilots grew considerably, and during the 1930s, a number of women held flying records.

By 1940, women were no longer oddities in any area of aviation. Be they stewardesses, engineers, businesswomen or pilots, they had, for the most part, accomplished their goals of making air travel a standard means of transportation and of proving

to the world that women could be competent pilots. The paths of succeeding women pilots, while still somewhat rocky, were smoothed in large measure by the enduring courage of women who were flying in the 1930s.

While the themes of aviation history are embedded within the broader framework of society, advances in flight technology have changed the course of human affairs. A particularly striking example is the airplane's impact on warfare, a theme that museum historians explored for the exhibition "Legend, Memory and the Great War in the Air." This exhibition examines the history of strategic bombing, first practiced in World War I and now an integral component of military strategy.

Similar questions will be addressed in the new Smithsonian History of Aviation Series, initiated by the museum's Department of Aeronautics. The series will provide a comprehensive examination of all facets of aviation history and will build a foundation for other research efforts. The series includes original research contributions and reprints of important historical works now out of print, as well as translations of articles and books that document the growth of aviation in other countries. The museum will also publish, as part of the series, important source documents such as rare government reports and previously unpublished items.

Gregg Herken, chairman of the Department of Space History, also completed, under the auspices of the Twentieth-Century Fund, a book on the science advisers of presidents, from Franklin Roosevelt to Ronald Reagan. His current research interest is the history of the nation's weapons laboratories at Los Alamos and Livermore.

In the United States, space-science research programs are the products of an increasingly complex process involving the federal government, private industry and universities. Many space research programs require vast sums of money and long-range planning, subjecting them to the vagaries of budget cuts and political compromises. Several historians in the Department of Space History study the administration and management of large-scale projects in the space program. This involves conducting oral and video history interviews with key participants in a given program and gathering the memos, letters, congressional testimony and other documents that chronicle such complex undertakings (see "Videohistory," Page 97).

Preliminary to this research, the project has initiated a systematic effort to identify, preserve and describe the records of the space program scattered among its industry, government and academic participants. The goal is to stimulate research that draws on a richer base of documentation, thereby allowing more comprehensive historical studies.

One extensively studied space-science project is the Hubble Space Telescope, the most ambitious and most costly scientific satellite ever built by the National Aeronautics and Space Administration. Launched aboard the space shuttle in 1990, the HST is supposed to peer farther into the heavens than the most powerful ground-based telescope, providing images 10 times more detailed. The instrument, even with some technical flaws, represents a multibillion-dollar scientific enterprise, one that survived uncertain budgets, cost overruns, early opposition from key legislators, missed schedules, launch delays and other obstacles.

In a cooperative undertaking involving the museum's Department of Space History and the History of Science Department at the Johns Hopkins University, museum historian Robert Smith and Joseph Tatarewicz, a historian then with the museum, traced the evolution of the Space Telescope. It was a tortuous process that began in the 1940s when a small group of astronomers first introduced the idea of a telescope in space. The historical investigations have yielded a wealth of documents and oral history interviews, permitting current and future researchers to analyze the complex decisions and interactions that influenced the making of the sophisticated instrument.

Contrasting the romantic image of the first air war with the hard realities of the war in the air and on the ground, the Air and Space Museum exhibition "Legend, Memory and the Great War in the Air" presents a new look at the first widespread military use of the airplane. (Photo by Carolyn Russo)

VIDEOHISTORY

The video camera is on trial at the Smithsonian. In a novel pilot program, researchers spent five years evaluating the video camera as a tool for documenting and studying the history of science and technology.

"This could be a research engine that serves all of the Smithsonian and its missions," says David DeVorkin, an adviser to the Smithsonian Videohistory Program.

In his work, DeVorkin, a member of the Department of Space History at the Air and Space Museum, found the video camera useful in documenting the actual process of doing science, particularly in fast-changing fields. A specialist in the history of astronomy, DeVorkin worked with the program's staff to videotape the Naval Observatory's Charles Worley, one of the last practitioners of "classical" observing techniques in astronomy.

As captured on videotape, Worley showed how astronomers in the not-so-distant past aimed their telescopes and observed celestial objects by peering through the eyepieces of their telescopes. Today, computers aim instruments, following a pre-programmed observing schedule, and data are collected not with the eye but with electronic instruments. For a curator of historically important instruments, videotaped renditions of how the equipment was used and, in some instances, how it was made provide valuable information.

When used to record group interviews, the camera can capture personal interactions that would otherwise go undocumented. "People sometimes challenge each other, and they expand on others' recollections and interpretations," program director Terri Schorzman says. One of the best examples, in Schorzman's view, is an animated and compelling interview with a group of wives of scientists who worked on the Manhattan Project during World War II.

That interview was one of many conducted by Stanley Goldberg, a consulting historian who is studying the development of the atomic bomb. To stimulate discussion and to illustrate the workings of complex equipment, many interviews were done at the facilities where parts of the bomb were made. "There is a lot of information in the video recordings that you don't find in other histories," Goldberg says.

During the project, Smithsonian historians interviewed more than 300 people on topics ranging from the history of X-ray astronomy to the development of the computer industry and the conservation of endangered species. The pilot program, which ended in 1991, was supported by a five-year grant from the Alfred P. Sloan Foundation in New York. ✳

In a Smithsonian videohistory documentation project, historian Stanley Goldberg (right) interviews physicists and Manhattan Project veterans K. T. Bambridge and R. R. Wilson, as they are videotaped by Dale Green in the New Mexico desert, where the first atomic bomb was tested in July 1945. (Photo by Phillip Seitz)

THROUGH
THE EYE OF
THE ARTIST

Stories Behind the Art

in Smithsonian Museums

*Grand western scenes such as Albert Bierstadt's "Among the Sierra
Nevada Mountains, California" (1868), detail, were re-examined
by the Museum of American Art in its landmark 1991 exhibition
"The West As America: Reinterpreting Images of the Frontier."*

This female figure and child, by the M'bembe peoples of Nigeria, and similar figures were once carved on one or both ends of the large slit drums that call people to ceremonies or to prepare for war. (Photo by Jeff Ploskonka)

Arthur Sackler, the late physician, medical publisher, art collector and Smithsonian benefactor, succinctly defined the distinction between two primary routes to understanding. "Art and science are two sides of the same coin," he wrote. "Science is a discipline pursued with passion. Art is a passion pursued with discipline."

Through the passion and the discipline of the artist, we are treated to the fruits of creativity. This may well be reward enough, but visual experience often stirs a desire to probe deeper, to become connected to the creator. What statement is the artist making and why? What experiences and influences—artistic, environmental and social—led to a particular artist's way of portraying the world?

Artworks, the products of individual expression, are also windows on society, sometimes mirroring prevailing styles, beliefs and attitudes, sometimes rejecting them. Thus, scholars studying the work of an artist who depended on the patronage of a ruling elite will learn of the symbolism, the concepts of beauty and the values of that elite. Technical analyses of aged works of art—for example, the examinations of paint pigments or the mineral content of clay in ceramics—yield insights into trade and other interactions between societies.

Works of art and their creators are themselves rich subjects of research, opening avenues of understanding closed to other areas of inquiry. Studies at the Smithsonian's eight art museums and its Archives of American Art (see "Stories Waiting to be Told," Page 103) are pursuing all of these avenues. Their broad and, in many ways, unique collections are also invaluable resources for thousands of art scholars and museum professionals each year.

History in Portraits

Even if you exclude the visage on the dollar bill, the most familiar face in the United States is that of George Washington. According to the Catalog of American Portraits, a project of the Smithsonian's National Portrait Gallery, he is the subject of thousands of artistic renderings. To be sure, several busts and portraits of the father of our nation can be found in the Portrait Gallery's collections. But the gallery also houses portraits and statues of other distinguished Americans who have left an imprint on our society. Included in the holdings are portrayals of the celebrated and the unjustly forgotten who helped shape the nation—in politics, science, business, and the arts and letters—along with folk heroes, entertainers, sports greats and many others.

A modern-day pantheon, the National Portrait Gallery reaches beyond capturing the best contemporary likenesses of people in American history. Images of presidents are not confined to official White House portraits. The collections include more than 1,600 covers of Time magazine; they also include a unique assemblage of the Mathew Brady photographs of the Civil War era, among them the cracked glass negative of the final photographic portrait of Abraham Lincoln made two days before his assassination. The collection encompasses irreverent caricatures of presidents and politicos created by noted editorial cartoonists over a 200-year span. In short, the Portrait Gallery's holdings are the fertile sources for the study of the nation's cultural and social history.

The gallery's research staff uses the biographical genre of portraiture as a vantage point for viewing American history. Curators and historians study the subjects of portraits, the artists who created the images and the relationships between subjects and artists. From this foundation, researchers can extend their inquiries into broader historical themes. The research specialties of staff members include the intellectual and cultural history of 18th- and 19th-century America, the history of American performing arts, the nation's cultural relationship with other countries at the turn of the century, and social and cultural aspects of American dress, to name a few.

The gallery's Peale Family Papers project combines many of these interests. Charles Willson Peale, the son of a London postal clerk who was banished to the Colonies for embezzling funds, painted more than 1,000 portraits of men and women of the Revolutionary War period, including George Washington, Thomas Jefferson, Ben-

jamin Franklin and Thomas Paine. The artist corresponded with these and other prominent Americans, discoursing on most aspects of social and political life in the young nation.

Like Franklin and Jefferson, Peale had multiple talents and interests. He was a gifted artist, but as his letters to Jefferson and others show, he was an inventor as well. His letters describe in fascinating detail his various mechanical creations, including a fan chair, a wooden-span bridge, a stove, a portable steam bath and a "polygraph," a device for making copies of writings.

Peale was also a pioneer and an innovator in the field of museums. He turned his Philadelphia home into a museum of natural history. It was not the first museum in the New World, but it was the first to depart from the traditional approach of museums as "cabinets of curiosities" wherein specimens were presented without the benefit of any underlying systematic rationale. Peale organized his collections to portray current understanding of the natural world. The museum was also unique

Images of all portraits in its collections, along with related information, have been entered into a videodisc system developed by the Portrait Gallery. The system has given easy access to information on the collections regardless of a researcher's geographical location. (Photo by Dane Penland)

One of few Colonial portraits depicting a woman in a professional role outside the home, Charles Willson Peale's circa 1769 painting of printer and publisher Anne Catharine Green is an important recent acquisition for the Portrait Gallery, which has a major research project on the Peale family.

entire collection of documents on microfiche, creating an invaluable resource for other historians. Project staff members have completed half of an eight-volume edition, *The Selected Papers of Charles Willson Peale and His Family,* that will reproduce about 2,000 of the documents. The Peales' annotated writings provide humanistic interpretations of events that shaped American society and its institutions, as well as first-person details of life in a middle-income family that emphasized intellectual and artistic enrichment.

A Home for American Art

The origins of the National Museum of American Art predate those of the Smithsonian itself. In 1829, John Varden, a well-to-do Washingtonian, began an art collection that he deemed fitting for the nation's capital. This collection was absorbed into the National Institute which displayed its works of art beside those belonging to the government in the third-floor galleries of the then-new Patent Office Building. In 1858, the collection belonging to the government was transferred to the Smithsonian, followed four years later by the National Institute collection.

Today, items in Varden's founding collection are among the more than 36,500 works of art—paintings, sculptures, prints, drawings, photographs and objects of folk art—in the museum's care. This collection of American art, including works by such greats as Thomas Cole, Mary Cassatt, Winslow Homer, Edward Hopper, Jacob Lawrence and Helen Frankenthaler, is the largest in the world. This fact, together with the museum's stature as a national institution and the quality of its scholarship, exhibitions and publications, makes the museum one of the world's leading centers for the study and display of American art. With its Renwick Gallery, devoted to the study and exhibition of American crafts and decorative arts, the museum addresses the full spectrum of American artistic pursuits, from Colonial times to the present.

The research activities of the museum's curators extend well beyond studies of the artworks themselves. The museum has developed seven computerized data bases that inventory more than 500,000 objects of American art. Assembled from information gathered by extensive survey networks that cover all 50 states, the data bases are invaluable resources for research, providing a thorough overview of American artistic traditions (see "Taking Inventory of the Nation's Art Heritage," Page 107). Each year, more than 2,000 researchers consult these resources.

for the day because it was not simply a repository, but an institution for the general public. Peale's museum marked an important advance in the nation's cultural and scientific development, coming at a time, 1786, when American scientists aspired to recognition as equals in the eyes of their European counterparts.

Since 1973, a team of researchers, directed by cultural historian Lillian B. Miller, has assembled and studied copies of nearly 6,000 letters, diaries and other writings of Charles Willson Peale and his family, including sons Raphaelle, Rembrandt, Rubens and Titian Ramsay, all of whom achieved prominence in artistic and scientific pursuits. Other Peale family members included in the research are Charles Willson Peale's nieces Sarah Miriam, Margaretta Angelica and Anna Claypoole, all daughters of Charles' brother James and all prominent artists as well. Spanning three generations, between 1735 and 1885, the family documents are a treasure of information on this period of American history. "If you are interested in the history of science and art in post-Revolutionary America," Miller says, "then you must know what Peale was doing."

Miller and her colleagues have reproduced the

STORIES WAITING TO BE TOLD

In 1954, when the Archives of American Art was founded in Detroit, the ranks of historians specializing in American art were terribly thin. As strange as it must seem today, not one chair in the field could be found on the faculty of a U.S. college or university.

The creation of the Archives was a major step toward correcting this imbalance. By acting to preserve primary source materials, the Archives ensured that historians would have the documentation needed to explore and interpret this integral part of the nation's cultural history.

The Archives, which became part of the Smithsonian in 1969, collects family and business correspondence, diaries, financial records of art galleries and organizations, sketchbooks, manuscripts of lectures and writings, photographs, scrapbooks, auction and exhibition catalogs, and tape-recorded interviews. The subjects of the continuing search for materials include not only the artists themselves but also dealers, critics, collectors, curators, historians and museums.

This bounty of raw historical information contains many untold stories about American art and American artists. "The Archives of American Art, acting as a matchmaker, brings documents and scholars together in the expectation that their offspring will be informative, accurate and well-written publications on the visual arts in America," senior curator emeritus Garnett McCoy has written.

The Archives' five regional offices—in New York City, Boston, Detroit, San Marino, and Washington, D.C.—have been prolific matchmakers. Tens of thousands of scholars have consulted the collections, and thousands of publications based on their research have been written about the history of American art.

The collection, which includes taped oral history interviews, has grown immensely—from 5 million documents in 1974 to today's total of more than 10 million items. Some of this material dates back to the early 18th century. ✳

Through the use of photographic slides, the Archives of American Art gives access to art projects, such as an outdoor Chicano mural project in California, when the works of art themselves cannot be collected. The mural (detail shown here), depicting the rise of the Chicano movement, was created in 1977 by a Chicano studies class under the direction of artists Patricia Rodríguez and Ray Patlán.

Recapturing a Past Glory

At the 1876 Centennial Exposition in Philadelphia, American artists fared poorly in juried competitions, fueling the European view that the United States was culturally backward. Defenders of American culture claimed that the poor showing reflected not the inferiority of American visual expression but rather the failure of American organizers to gather the works of the nation's best artists. But for American artists themselves, the argument was not convincing. In the exposition's aftermath, according to George Gurney, art historian at the Museum of American Art, hundreds of American artists journeyed to Europe, where they sought technical training and philosophical enrichment.

Nearly two decades later, at the 1893 Columbian Exposition in Chicago, the nation aspired to show the world that it had ascended to the status of an equal in all realms of culture. So pervasive was this ambition that historian Henry Brooks Adams characterized the world's fair as a watershed in American culture. The selections by regional juries—involving nearly 1,200 works by 521 artists, including Thomas Eakins, John Singer Sargent, Cecilia Beaux, James McNeill Whistler, George Innes, John La Farge, Winslow Homer—appeared at the exposition. "Chicago," Adams wrote, "was the first expression of American thought as unity...."

The spirit and reality of that accomplishment was recaptured in 1993 in a joint exhibition of the Museum of American Art and the Portrait Gallery, which share the magnificent old Patent Office Building. Researchers of the two museums assembled a representative sample of about 100 American paintings and sculptures originally displayed at the Chicago exposition. As part of this effort, Gurney and his colleagues embarked on an effort to locate all of the paintings and sculptures displayed in the fair's American art section.

Before the project began, the whereabouts of only a few hundred works were known. Searches through old newspaper articles, obituaries, art-auction catalogs, social registers and other historical materials added steadily to the total. Some works, the researchers found, had been destroyed. If they could not locate the actual work, the researchers tried at least to find a picture of the lost painting or sculpture.

Fair planners, Gurney notes, used art to symbolize the emergence of a "national culture ... art intersected with significant social movements of the day." Inevitably, then, exhibition-related studies and publications explore how closely prevailing artistic values reflected these movements.

None of this would come as a total surprise to the author of *The Book of the Fair,* who wrote in 1893, "A hundred years hence it may be that this Exposition will itself be deemed worthy of a celebration...."

An Enigmatic American Master

A notable omission at the Columbian Exposition was Albert Pinkham Ryder, the reclusive artist whom many regard as the greatest American painter. Ryder's legacy includes about 160 paintings—landscapes and rural scenes, marine subjects and spiritual themes—and endless conjecture about his life, painting techniques and artistic influences.

Because so little is known about Ryder, because the shadow of his influence is so large, researchers at the Museum of American Art—which owns 16

Hirshhorn Museum exhibition curator Judith Zilczer examines paintings by Willem de Kooning in the museum's storage area in preparation for a major exhibition of the artist's work. (Photo by Jeff Tinsley)

of his works—joined with the Smithsonian's Conservation Analytical Laboratory in a major study to define the master in the context of his times. This was a complex task for several reasons. First, Ryder's published writing consists of just 10 paragraphs—a lyrical, mystical explanation of his unhurried approach to painting. Next, the number of forgeries of Ryder's works exceeds his total production. And finally, Ryder's use of unconventional materials—tobacco juice and candle grease, among others—combined with his experimental methods render his paintings susceptible to cracking and other damage; a number of his paintings have undergone extensive conservation and restoration, sometimes so extensive as to obscure the artist's own work.

The research team was led by museum director Elizabeth Broun, who has noted that "Ryder's art and life are a cornerstone of 20th-century modernism, the first American steps toward an artistic avant-garde." The study exploited advanced scientific techniques to retrace the evolution of selected Ryder paintings and in order to learn more about his methods and to gain insight into his creativity.

The scientific analyses were performed by Conservation Analytical Laboratory staff members. The skilled efforts of the lab's physicists, chemists and other scientists revealed preliminary sketches, individual brush strokes, reworked areas and details of the master's technique.

Some of these studies were carried out at the research reactor of the National Institute of Standards and Technology in Gaithersburg, Md., where CAL shares the use of a variety of scientific instruments. The Smithsonian is the only U.S. institution to use a research reactor for neutron activation in studies of art history and related topics. This is normally the province of materials scientists.

The blending of art and science can be a productive endeavor. Consider the technique known as autoradiography. In this technique, a painting is subjected to a beam of neutrons; the pigments and other materials of the painting become slightly radioactive, revealing images of the distribution of the materials. The activated elements decay at different rates, and beta particles are emitted and recorded on radiographic film. The entire process takes about two months.

For Broun and Ingrid Alexander, an art research historian at CAL, autoradiographs—much like X-ray radiographs—of Ryder's works held information on the materials he used, how he initially approached a subject, how his ideas changed, and other questions related to the artist's techniques and

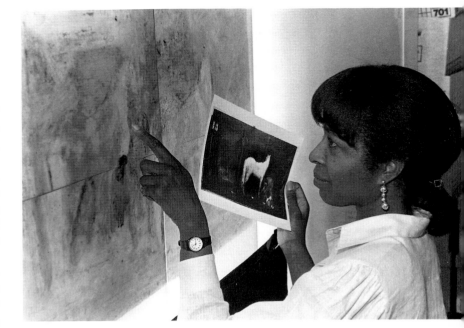

intentions. For example, autoradiographs of one painting, "In the Stable," which was completed around 1890, reveal the figure of a young stable boy who does not appear in the completed work. Apparently, too, Ryder labored over the horse in the work; the autoradiographs showed that he painted three horse heads before settling on the final image.

The technical study is helping to resolve a long-standing debate over Ryder's technique, which has been described as "lonely, experimental, in a sense, perverse." Some critics, Broun notes, go further and describe Ryder as "naive," ignorant of proper procedures that would have spared his thickly layered paintings from the threat of severe deterioration. "The implication is that he would have used traditional methods had he known them," Broun says. "Yet, Ryder's own words, and those of his friends, suggest that he was consciously experimenting with color, seeking a new and richer effect."

Seeing the World with New Perspectives

Strange things happen after dark. Perhaps that is why artist Krzysztof Wodiczko used the darkness of evening some years back to emblazon a disarming image on the circular facade of the Smithsonian's Hirshhorn Museum and Sculpture Garden. Projected onto the side of the building facing the National Mall were two huge hands—one brandishing a revolver, the other holding a candle. Positioned between these arresting photo projections, below a broad seatlike balcony, was another projection showing a bank of enormous microphones as if set up for a giant's news conference.

Research art historian Ingrid Alexander of the Conservation Analytical Laboratory examines autoradiographs of a painting by 19th-century artist Albert Pinkham Ryder. (Photo by Doc Dougherty)

This exercise in creativity was, of course, subjective. Equally, each viewer had to decide for himself or herself just what set of messages was being projected to a world burdened by aimless violence and media hype. But speak these images did, for even the most hurried pedestrians stopped to stare.

The novel exhibition was created specifically for the Hirshhorn Museum as part of its "WORKS" program, which showcased the creativity of promising young artists. "WORKS" demonstrated that today's art world is distinguished by experimentation, a search for new languages of expression, and that the Hirshhorn, as a premier museum of modern and contemporary art, is ready to encourage such bold experimentation. At the same time, the museum is grounded in scholarship; in its research and exhibitions, the Hirshhorn reaches back in time to the origins of modern painting and sculpture. It was no accident that, while the Wodiczko-created images were projected onto the museum's exterior, a retrospective of the trail-blazing work of the early 20th-century sculptor Alberto Giacometti was on view inside.

Unlike Rembrandts or El Grecos, many of the museum's works of art have not been examined and documented by generations of scholars. Each exhibition at the Hirshhorn, curator of paintings Judith K. Zilczer notes, is a new scholarly enterprise. The assembly of each new exhibition requires pioneering research and analysis. The result is not only a thought-provoking exhibition but also a catalog that becomes a valuable research tool for current scholars, as well as future generations of art historians.

The Hirshhorn Museum and Sculpture Garden is named for benefactor Joseph H. Hirshhorn, a remarkable self-made man, who, over the course of several decades, gathered a comprehensive and star-studded collection of works beginning with the latter part of the 19th century. The museum, which opened in 1974, features a collection of some 12,500 works of art documenting the contributions of modern art from the spread of impressionism and cubism to reinventions of realism to abstract expressionism and beyond. The giants who changed the way we look at the world over the past century are all in the Hirshhorn's collections. Monumental sculptures by Alexander Calder, Henry Moore, Claes Oldenburg and Auguste Rodin, among others, are displayed in the sculpture garden on the National Mall. The sculpture collection also includes works by Henri Matisse, Raymond Duchamp-Villon, Edward and Nancy Kienholz, Gaston Lachaise, Aristide Maillol, David Smith and Bruce Nauman.

The painting collection traces the history of 20th-century American painting through works by such artists as Horace Pippin, Robert Henri, Edward Hopper, Jackson Pollock, Morris Louis, Larry Rivers and Susan Rothenberg. The contributions of immigrant artists to modern American art are represented in works by such artists as Josef Albers, Arshile Gorky and Willem de Kooning. Also included in the collection are paintings by leading modern artists in Europe and Latin America: Joan Miró, Jean Dubuffet, Fernando Botero and Anselm Kiefer, among others.

Contact with the artist himself and with the private galleries that display his work helped strengthen a Hirshhorn retrospective of the work of the British painter Francis Bacon, a powerful technician and a sometimes savage commentator on the human condition who died in 1992. Tracking down some of the paintings needed to represent phases in Bacon's career, Zilczer says, "took a little bit of detective work." The museum's director, James Demetrion, who had developed a deep knowledge of Bacon's art from following his work and career for many years, organized the show with Zilczer's assistance. They relied on records of both the artist and his dealer in order to find several paintings that had not been on public view for decades. The show became a blockbuster hit.

To buttress a major exhibition, the Hirshhorn Museum typically holds related events that also go on to become part of the scholarly product. Transcripts of interviews with the artist might become part of the museum's research resources, along with taped lectures and other public education programs.

One of the primary responsibilities of Hirshhorn curators is to maintain and build a "collection archive" for each artwork in the collection. The archive includes all documentation for the given work and may also include interviews with the artist, questionnaires that give firsthand accounts of an artist's biography and other relevant material. Standards have been developed for gathering complete documentation for specific types of art. With sculpture, for example, curators attempt to document all known variations of a given piece.

As a modern art museum, the Hirshhorn must be concerned with today, as well as yesterday. The "fieldwork" of Hirshhorn curators, Zilczer says, consists of keeping abreast of what's happening right now, studying the ever-changing art market, following the exhibitions of leading commercial galleries, visiting artists' studios both in this country and abroad. By serving on jury panels for regional

The Smithsonian's bureaus take their designation as national museums quite literally. The ambitious inventorying programs initiated by the National Portrait Gallery and the National Museum of American Art are examples of a commitment to the nation.

Since 1966, at the Portrait Gallery, staff members of the Catalog of American Portraits have been tracking down portraits in public and private collections in all 50 states. To date, they have collected—through mail surveys and on-site investigations—documentation and photographs of more than 80,000 likenesses of historically important Americans. The catalog grows almost daily. It includes lists of paintings, drawings, sculptures, miniatures and silhouettes along with biographical information on the artists and their subjects. Cross-referenced to aid all types of historical study, the catalog is a unique visual and textual record of people who have participated in the nation's historical development.

Four years after this program began, the Museum of American Art set out to identify all American paintings completed before 1914. The Inventory of American Paintings has yielded a still-growing lode of valuable information. Thus far, some 250,000 paintings by 22,000 artists have been identified and listed in a computerized data base. Among these paintings were lost treasures, masterpieces whose whereabouts had been unknown. Surveying efforts uncovered, for example, six paintings by Arthur B. Davies in an Indiana high school. "Mist Offshore" by William Merritt Chase and a portrait of Washington attributed to Gilbert Stuart were also found.

Many of these paintings, of course, do not qualify as masterpieces, but even the creations of the most obscure artists are threads woven into the nation's cultural fabric. As a whole, the works and artists listed in the Inventory of American Paintings, which adds some 10,000 new entries annually, chronicle changes in

artistic expression and technique, as well as changes in American tastes, lifestyles and attitudes toward art. The inventory can inspire comparative studies—investigations, for instance, of regional tastes or artistic influences over time—that otherwise might not be possible.

Building on the success of its painting inventory, the Museum of American Art has launched a major program funded by the Pew Charitable Trusts, the Henry Luce Foundation and the Getty Grant Program, among others, to identify all sculpture created by American artists. In addition to documenting museum and private collections, the survey aims to account for works of sculpture scattered about the American landscape, at sites that range from battlefields to traffic islands. ✹

Smithsonian volunteers test survey methods in preparation for Save Outdoor Sculpture!—a joint project of the Museum of American Art and the National Institute for the Conservation of Cultural Property. This sculpture, "Scenes From Shakespeare," by John Gregory, can be seen outside the Folger Shakespeare Library in Washington, D.C. (Photo by Rick Vargas)

art exhibitions, the curators keep up to date on the art scene outside of the major urban centers such as New York City and Los Angeles. "We're dealing with real people and real careers," Zilczer says.

Hirshhorn curators work with promising young artists, developing temporary exhibitions that expose visitors to new talent. One exhibition series, "Directions," focuses on individual contemporary artists. One such exhibition, "Keith Sonnier: Neon," called attention to the artist's use of a wide variety of media to evoke cultural, psychological and mystical associations. His glowing neon creations build upon the dada and surrealist tradition of collage and assemblage. "I have an intense interest in primitive cultures, anthropologically, sociologically, politically," Sonnier says, "but when it comes to actually making work, I feel that I have to contain my information in a real 20th-century machine-age context."

Naturally, the Hirshhorn's director and the curators constantly re-evaluate the collection to see what's missing and strive to fill in the gaps that exist even in so strong a body of work. They work to ensure that all important artists from a particular period are represented, for example, or that appropriate works from each stage in a particular artist's career are included.

That is no easy task. Even though the art boom of the '80s has ended, prices are still high, particularly for a museum with a limited acquisitions budget. As a result, each acquisition takes on greater significance, and accession strategies, designed to enhance the balance and importance of public collections, become more important.

Spanning Seven Millennia

The Arthur M. Sackler Gallery and the Freer Gallery of Art are neighbors on the National Mall and together form one of the world's pre-eminent centers for the study of Asian art and culture. The collections of the two museums span seven millennia and encompass the entire region, from the shores of the Mediterranean to the islands of Japan.

Studies carried out by the museums' combined staff and by visiting scholars strive to make the brilliance and diversity of Asian art—for example, Chinese bronzes and jades, Buddhist and Hindu sculptures, Indian miniatures and Japanese screens—better-known to the American public. In so doing, the researchers add to Western understanding of the cultures and histories of the peoples of Asia, home to more than half the world's population.

Brilliantly colored with opaque watercolor, ink and gold, this double-page composition from Iran, "A Prince Enthroned Surrounded by Attendants," dates from about 1425 and is part of the Vever collection of the Sackler Gallery.

An Aesthetic Rendering of History

"Art, whether one practices it or loves it," wrote Henri Vever, Parisian jeweler, art collector and painter, "gives gratifications that directly refresh and delight the soul." Vever died in 1942; the collection of Islamic art of the 11th through the 18th centuries, which he passionately and skillfully assembled, lives on in Washington.

Through a fortuitous series of events, the incomparable Vever Collection is now among the holdings of the Sackler Gallery. The collection vanished during World War II, a suspected casualty of the Nazi occupation of France. For decades no one knew where it was or if it still existed. But then a chance meeting between the collection's owner and a curator's mother in 1986 led, in time, to the Smithsonian's purchase of the nearly 500 paintings, illuminated manuscripts and bookbindings. Unlike other early collections of Persian art that have been sold off piecemeal, the Vever Collection, with its works of elegance, expressive intimacy and technical brilliance, and its significant examples of Islamic cultural history, remains intact.

The high esteem that Islamic culture has bestowed on books begins with the Koran, Islam's holy scripture. Regarded as the manifestation of divine power, the Koran records the revelations received by the prophet Muhammad in the early seventh century. As reverence for the Koran spread to other expressions of the written word, books became central to Islamic intellectual life and the highly prized possessions of the aristocracy. Among the ruling elite, book patronage rivaled building as a royal activity. In the richly illustrated manuscripts of the Vever Collection, historians can explore nine centuries of Islamic culture and society.

The Vever Collection is richest in Persian works. It includes illustrated pages from several versions of the *Shahnama,* an epic poem that recounts the history of Iran, from its first mythical kings to the downfall of the Sasanians in the middle of the seventh century. Though fewer in number, works from India in the collection are also important additions to the artistic and historical record. Among them are more than a dozen pages from the *Late Shahjahan Album,* a collection of paintings and calligraphies assembled in 1650 for the emperor who built the Taj Mahal.

The pages from Indian manuscripts are "very descriptive," says Milo Beach, director of the two galleries and a specialist in Indian and Islamic art. "They describe textiles, how people tied their turbans, how they wore their clothes. It's something that gives us a great deal of information about the people and, consequently, helps us to see their lives—to understand them, to understand a different culture and a different time period."

Typical of the interdisciplinary research on the collections of the paired galleries is the examination of the Vever Collection that yielded a two-volume publication with essays on Henri Vever's aesthetic and intellectual interests and on new approaches to the study of Persian painting, plus an annotated checklist that included scientific analysis of the works. As a part of that effort, Elisabeth West FitzHugh, a now-retired conservation scientist in the galleries' Department of Conservation and Scientific Research, studied paint pigments from a representative sample of 32 paintings. Her microchemical analyses and review of historical references produced new information—for example, greens are usually mixtures of yellow pigment and blue indigo, and purples are combinations of white, blue and red, rather than being a single purple pigment as had been previously assumed. A related investigation by her colleague Janet Douglas focused on the papers used for illustration and calligraphy, providing new information on the history of papermaking in the Near East.

A Modern Master of Chinese Painting

Like nearly all students of Chinese painting, Chang Dai-chien began his career by studying and imitating the ancient masters. But unlike most aspiring Chinese artists, who tend to specialize in only one painting genre, Chang became accomplished in all major categories of Chinese painting—landscapes, figures, animals, birds and flowers. He became so accomplished, in fact, that private and public collections around the world contain paintings that are attributed to ancient masters but which are actually the work of Chang, who was born near the turn of the 20th century.

Chang Dai-chien, creator of an estimated 30,000 paintings over a 60-year career, was the subject of a major study by Shen C. Y. Fu, senior curator of Chinese art at the Sackler and Freer galleries. Fu, whose research culminated in a retrospective exhibition of Chang's work at the Sackler, examined Chang's development from an imitator of ancient masters to an original creator of bold, kinesthetic landscapes that forged new directions in Chinese art.

During the last two decades of his life, Fu explains, Chang departed from the highly detailed imagery characteristic of much traditional Chinese painting and adopted a freer style that brought him fame as a "modern" painter. Even during this pe-

REVISITING THE FABULOUS PEACOCK ROOM

Ever since the Freer Gallery of Art opened in May 1923, visitors have marveled at James McNeill Whistler's striking specimen of interior design known as "Harmony in Blue and Gold: The Peacock Room."

Permanently installed in the Freer's southeast corner, the 20-by-32-foot room is the only surviving interior scheme of this towering and influential American painter. Whistler spent most of his career in England, and the Peacock Room is the pre-eminent decoration of the English aesthetic movement.

The enthralling story of its development begins in 1876 when the domineering shipping magnate Frederick Leyland commissioned architect Thomas Jeckyll to decorate the dining room of his new London townhouse. Jeckyll was charged with accommodating some of Leyland's most prized possessions—a collection of Chinese blue-and-white porcelain; some 16th-century leather wall hangings, said to have belonged to Catherine of Aragon; and Whistler's painting, "The Princess From the Land of Porcelain." Above a walnut wainscot, Jeckyll installed a framework to support both the leather hangings and a lattice of shelving. He topped the room with a fan-vaulted Jacobean ceiling. Having almost completed the project, Jeckyll consulted Whistler about the color scheme, and the transformation of the room began.

Leyland, Whistler's long-time patron, sanctioned the painter's proposal for minor alterations. When the magnate left town for the summer, Whistler painted over the prized leather wall hangings and every other surface, transforming Jeckyll's scheme into one entirely of his own invention. Whistler took his inspiration from the peacock, and his six large gold images of that exotic bird dominate the room, along with his painting of "The Princess."

Whistler's initiative caused a permanent rift between the artist and his patron, but the Peacock Room came to be regarded in England and America as a magnificent masterpiece of design.

Then, in 1904, Charles Lang Freer, an American collector, particularly of works by Whistler, purchased the Peacock Room and arranged for its installation in his Detroit home. When Freer died in 1919, the room was transported to Washington and installed in the Freer Gallery.

But as years passed, the colorful brilliance and structural soundness of the Peacock Room suffered. In 1947, the Freer hired a team of restoration practitioners, the Finlayson brothers of Boston, to restabilize, clean and restore it. Now, painting conservators have just completed work on a two-year, $300,000 research and conservation project to restore the masterpiece to its former splendor. The Peacock Room project was part of a major renovation of the Freer that created new conservation laboratories and newly reinstalled galleries.

The room was structurally secure, but the most recent conservation project showed that the Finlaysons, confined by the techniques and attitudes of their time, skewed the balance of the room. The recent treatment aimed at restoring the harmony between "fine arts" and "decorative" elements that was central to Whistler's vision. The work was carried out by a team from the University of Delaware/Winterthur Art Conservation Program in association with expert Freer staff.

The Finlaysons paid most attention to the peacock images on the shutters and the wall. The "frames" created by the wainscoting, shelves and ceiling were equally important to Whistler's ideas. The Finlaysons gave minimal treatment to the shelves and masked the original brushwork and color harmonies of the ceiling with "gilt paint and oil colors applied with a brush and a wadded rag to match existing decoration," according to a few surviving notes.

Whistler's methods were technically complex. He chose unusual materials, such as copper resinate, which served as an adhesive for Dutch metal leaf to create the distinctive transparent green-gold that appears on many of the surfaces in the room. The effect was painted over or ignored in the Finlaysons' restoration.

Whistler's distinctive use of materials, which also included Prussian-blue paint, gold leaf, and gold and platinum pigment—often combined on such surfaces as wood, canvas and leather—presented conservators with a variety of concerns. Whistler worked and reworked his surfaces and in some parts of the room created as many as 13 layers of paint and varnish.

As the conservators removed the discolored varnish and paint applied by the Finlaysons, they had to devise ways to assure that the original layers were not harmed. This is an issue common to most painting conservation projects, but it was intensified in the Peacock Room because different cleaning systems had to be selected to preserve the many types and combinations of media Whistler used.

Fortuitously, a team member, Richard Wolbers, had been a molecular biologist at the Salk Institute before switching careers. He has pioneered the application of biomedical research techniques to the organic aspects of painting conservation. "A lot of medical technology," Wolbers says, "is easily applicable to paint."

The team removed tiny paint samples—about half the size of the head of a pin—from different parts of the room. Taking cross sections of the samples, they used the fluorescent stains that Wolbers had borrowed from biochemistry to identify the types of organic substances used by Whistler. With this information, they developed treatment plans for each area of the room.

Infrared and ultraviolet photography has also played an important role in the project. The conservators used these diagnostic techniques and photomicrography to show the extent and place-

ment of overpainting in the first restoration of the room.

The project has provided scientific evidence about Whistler's organization of materials. These facts have clarified—and, in some cases, contradicted—existing anecdotal accounts and can be used to reinterpret Whistler's aesthetic ambitions. A new view of the history of the Peacock Room has resulted. Equally, or more, important, the Peacock Room is restored to all its glory for the benefit of new generations of museumgoers. ✳

Conservators Joyce Hill Stoner (left) and Wendy Samet remove a tiny paint sample from a shutter in the Freer Gallery's Peacock Room and document the procedure. (Photo by John Tsantes)

In a joint international project between the Museum of African Art and the National Museum of Mali, Smithsonian curator Philip Ravenhill worked with film-maker Stanley Staniski (with camera) to document Dogon and Bamana art. (Photo by Philip Ravenhill)

riod, however, Chang's "classical roots were still important," Fu maintains, "and the ancient 'splashed ink' technique of Chinese painting shaped his more abstract works."

Adamantly opposed to the Communist government that established itself in China in 1949, Chang spent the last 34 years of his life in voluntary exile, living in Hong Kong, India, Japan, Europe, Argentina, Brazil, California and, finally, Taiwan. These critical life changes are reflected in the evolution of his painting style and theory of art. "The new scenery and people he met, including Picasso, influenced his development," Fu says.

Through research, Fu retraced the artist's odyssey, established the Chinese and Western context of Chang's career, dated all of the painter's known works on the basis of stylistic analysis and reviewed Chang's published writings on art, Fu's surviving personal correspondence and the inscriptions that appear on many of his paintings. Like much else in the work of the two galleries, Fu's exhibition catalog, with major contributions and translated by Jan Stuart, assistant curator of Chinese art, along with the exhibition itself, helps to promote better cultural understanding between East and West.

The Powers and Mysteries of African Art

In the United States, the Smithsonian's National Museum of African Art is the only museum devoted exclusively to studying, collecting and exhibiting African art. The museum assumes a leading role in fostering understanding of the continent's diverse cultures and artistic achievements, with particular emphasis on the vast sub-Saharan region.

The museum's research program is an essential supporting element of this mission. Through exhibitions, books and articles, and educational programs, chief curator Philip Ravenhill says, research at the museum aims to ensure that "African art becomes part of everyone's artistic consciousness."

Interest in Africa has increased considerably in recent years. But most Westerners have less than a nodding acquaintance with the visual traditions of Africa's peoples. This despite the fact that, in the early part of the century, European artists and critics elevated one of Africa's primary art forms—sculpture—from purely ethnographic and curiosity status to a recognized and admired art form. For the "discoverers" of African art in the early 1900s, the museum's associate director, Roy Sieber, explains, the exotic forms in unfamiliar styles and strange proportions—oversized heads, squat bodies, frontal poses and often symmetrical gestures—became a refreshingly new alternative to Asian traditions and European classicism and naturalism.

The museum's research programs and exhibitions concentrate on the aesthetic qualities of African art forms, but they also explore the development and meaning of the arts. Such a comprehensive view of African visual traditions—one that integrates works of high artistic merit with their historical and cultural underpinnings—has been lacking for most of this century. Even today, African art is a neglected area of scholarly inquiry. Only a third of U.S. colleges and universities with doctoral programs in art history offer courses in African art, and far fewer offer graduate degrees.

The artistic traditions of the many peoples who live south of the Sahara are infused with cultural meanings that invest art objects with distinct social, political and religious meaning.

Unlike colleagues who study other regions of the world, African art scholars face formidable obstacles in reconstructing the history of art objects. Because most African artworks are made of wood and other organic materials that decay rapidly in sub-Saharan climates, few predate the 19th century. Objects of stone, metal and fired clay recovered from archaeological digs are rare. An equally important factor is the contextual role of African art. Made to be used, many objects are eventually broken or destroyed or worn out. Replacements are accorded the same cultural and symbolic value as the originals; however, despite their conformity with traditional style and form, they are not exact copies.

The famous copper alloy works from Benin were removed from Africa during the British Punitive Expedition of 1897. After leaving Africa, these magnificent works—plaques, commemorative heads, hip masks and other objects made between the 14th and 19th centuries—were subjected to a variety of surface treatments when they entered museum, dealer and private collections in Europe. Today, some of these surfaces are discolored by these treatments and, therefore, do not represent the original Benin aesthetic. Postdoctoral fellow Dr. Janet Schrenk spent two years investigating the collection at the Museum of African Art in order to help museum conservators develop appropriate treatments to rescue these precious works.

Little is known about individual African artists. Recorded information is scarce, and the records of European collectors during the colonial period often neglected to identify and collect data about artists.

One artist whose name is known is the master sculptor Olowe of Ise, Nigeria, who died in 1938. An elaborately carved wooden door panel, from a Yoruba palace, recently donated to the museum, is one of the many works by Olowe being examined by curator Roslyn Walker. Her research on the artist and his oeuvre will result in the first monograph devoted to a traditional African artist. "Olowe's carving style is distinctive, characterized by a delicate attenuation of forms," Walker says. Researchers like Walker also consider the role of African patrons, who often negotiated with artists on the style and form of commissioned objects. Thus, researchers find it necessary to conduct fieldwork, interviewing artists and patrons and documenting the uses and meanings ascribed to art objects, as well as reconstructing the original contents of the works.

A fertile source of additional research is the museum's Eliot Elisofon Photographic Archives, which contains 200,000 color slides; 78,000 black-and-white photographs; and 140,000 feet of motion picture film and videotape. Named for the famed Life magazine photographer, the Elisofon Archives also preserves many historical images, as well as the visual materials of recent field investigators.

African Art from the Inside and Outside

Among the distinguishing features of African art objects are the multiple meanings ascribed to them. "The meaning of a work of art was assigned by the culture on the basis of form and subject matter and the manner in which it was used," Sieber says. "But it is accessible only from information from its original users."

In "African Art in the Cycle of Life," a major museum exhibition in 1987–1988, Sieber and curator Walker carefully selected 84 objects to demonstrate the many threads that link art and society. They examined how sub-Saharan groups use art to commemorate the events and stages of life. For example, masks and headdresses—often the incarnation of ancestors or nature spirits—are worn during coming-of-age ceremonies, agricultural and healing rituals, and funerals. Jewelry and other personal adornments shown in the exhibition illustrated how these objects distinguish status, age and gender, and how they strengthen communal solidarity.

Understanding how these works of art were used, Sieber argues, invests them with a "cultural reality" that underscores their aesthetic power.

values, as well as power.... The frequency with which these depictions appear is not the issue. Rather, how each icon functioned in varying contexts and how artists conceived them through time are of paramount concern."

A National Museum of Design

The Cooper-Hewitt, National Museum of Design, a Smithsonian bureau since 1968, was founded in 1897 as a working resource, a visual index to the history of the design arts. Located in New York City, the museum now occupies Andrew Carnegie's Georgian-style mansion and a neighboring townhouse—gifts of the Carnegie Corp. to house the museum and its superb collections. Wall coverings, decorative art objects, textiles, and prints and drawings constitute the nucleus of this world-famous center for the study of design. The museum's permanent collection represents the cultures of Europe, America, Asia and other regions of the world over a span of 3,000 years. The museum now seeks particularly to build its collections of 19th- and 20th-century design, including examples of contemporary urban and industrial design. The museum's library—which houses 50,000 volumes, including 5,000 rare books and archives on color, pattern, symbols, advertising, and industrial and interior design—echoes the themes of the collections and serves as a unique resource for scholars and designers alike. The museum also has an extensive education program, including graduate work in the history of the decorative arts.

The textile collections at the Cooper-Hewitt span an impressive range in geography and time. Though focusing mainly on textiles produced in Western Europe from the 13th century up to today, the museum also holds textiles from the Han dynasty of China dating back to roughly the third century B.C., as well as examples of Coptic and Islamic textiles.

Research on this collection, Milton Sonday, the museum's curator of textiles, says, can be broken down into several principal areas: the analysis and understanding of technique, be it weaving, dyeing and printing, or lace making; the history and meaning of motifs; or social and historical contexts. The museum's goal is two-fold: to understand the history of textiles, including methods of production and aesthetic values reflected in pattern designs, and to document these aspects of the historical and modern textile industry.

The museum's location is ideal, providing access to the textile industry, largely headquartered in

David McFadden, curator of decorative arts at the Cooper-Hewitt Museum, works with design objects from the museum's collections, which include both historic and contemporary objects. (Photo by Rex Nobles)

He cautions, however, against explaining African art solely on the basis of its cultural context. Rather, he says, cultural information and historical data help to make the aesthetics and creativity of the artist "comprehensible to a viewer from another culture."

Cross-cultural comparisons also foster deeper levels of understanding of both African art and the culturally acquired predispositions of the viewer. "Icons: Ideals and Power in the Art of Africa," another exhibition at the museum, explored five types of imagery that are shared by many African groups and, indeed, Western cultures, among them, figures of the woman-child, the couple, the aggressive male hunter or warrior, and the rider. As director Sylvia Williams stated in the exhibition catalog, "Their meanings are often multivalent—religious, social and political—but all are expressive of ideas and

Manhattan. The 20th-century textile collection, in addition to tracing changes in styles, documents some of the radical changes that have taken place such as the emergence of the fiber artist in the United States in the late 1950s and the use of faster production equipment, including roller-screen printing and automated looms. Sonday points out that the collection of hand- and commercially printed, painted and woven fabrics of the past two decades is particularly strong and includes fabrics produced in the United States, Europe, Scandinavia, Japan, Australia and other countries for both home and personal use.

The largest portion of Cooper-Hewitt's collections consists of prints and drawings, with more than 100,000 individual items. In addition to artists' drawings, the collection includes designs for the theater, architectural drawings and designs for an immense variety of objects, ranging from the base of a crucifix to clocks, inkwells, gunmounts and furniture. Most materials are designs from 18th-century Europe. One of the museum's most recent acquisitions, however, was the invaluable archive of some 2,500 drawings and documentary material of the influential modernist American industrial designer Donald Deskey.

Cooper-Hewitt's decorative arts collection encompasses a range of three-dimensional objects, loosely categorized as ceramics, metalwork, glass and furniture, as well as plastics, industrial design, jewelry and diverse collections such as buttons and matchsafes. Industrial design does not include large-scale machines, but focuses on objects designed particularly for personal and domestic use. There are no clear-cut acquisition boundaries, says David McFadden, curator of decorative arts. "We are interested in the unusual, as well as the typical, in our documentary collections," he says, "not just in an object's style or value."

And by constantly reviewing the objects in the collections, McFadden says, scholars are able to deepen their knowledge of design principles and practices across the centuries. Often, that work means re-examining processes of production or learning how the introduction of new techniques or materials expanded the creative range of design. This means, too, that in our changing technological world the museum must keep track of new materials and new manufacturing processes that may have an impact on design.

The Cooper-Hewitt Museum brought together, from around the world, fabrics rich in the reflection of current decorative arts and design, as well as technological advances. The resulting research led to this 1991 exhibition, "Color, Light, Surface: Contemporary Fabrics." (Photo by Jennifer Kotter)

STEWARDSHIP OF THE NATION'S COLLECTIONS

A Glimpse of How

We Preserve Our Heritage

Greg Brass, a member of the Salteaux tribe of Canada, inventories American Indian artifacts in the storage areas of the Museum of Natural History, using both written and photographic documentation. (Photo by Richard Strauss)

Hundreds of containers of fish and other aquatic life, above and opposite, in the "wet" collections of the Museum of Natural History have been transferred to the Museum Support Center in Suitland, Md., where they are kept in controlled environments for the use of researchers. (Photos by Doc Dougherty)

As keeper of the national collections, the Smithsonian has a unique responsibility to protect and conserve each and every one of nearly 140 million objects. Researchers, students and other scholars work with these objects knowing that they are temporary stewards, gleaning information from an artifact, artwork or specimen while remaining aware that the collections are held in trust for the American people and for future generations of scholars.

Most artifacts are donated to the Institution by individuals, private collectors and such federal agencies as the National Aeronautics and Space Administration. Thousands of items come to the Smithsonian through field expeditions, bequests, purchases, and exchanges with other museums and organizations. Curators seek objects—everything from works of art to zoological specimens—that are appropriate to their particular museums. The basic guidelines for collecting an object include its authenticity and its historic, artistic, technical or scientific significance.

The Smithsonian accepts—accessions, as museum people say—only those items that truly fill a gap in the national collections and then only after careful consideration by museum curators, collections managers and directors. Because of this rigorous selection process, the Institution adds to the collections only a tiny percentage of what it is offered.

Storing Carefully to Preserve

At the museums on the National Mall, artworks, natural history specimens and artifacts are stored in behind-the-scenes areas where temperature, humidity and light levels are controlled. Access to these storage and research areas is limited to staff, research associates and visiting researchers.

The National Air and Space Museum has 16 collection storage buildings at the Paul E. Garber Facility in Suitland, Md., about six miles from the National Mall. There, the museum houses and restores airplanes, spacecraft and associated artifacts. Four of the buildings are open to the public by appointment for docent-led tours, and an open house for the public is held once every two years.

Managing the Collections

Suitland is also home to the Museum Support Center, a facility dedicated to collections management rather than exhibition. Since its opening in 1983, the building has provided modern storage and security for the national collections, as well as office and laboratory space. Because of a shortage of storage space in the museums—especially two of the largest, the National Museum of Natural History and the National Museum of American History—the Museum Support Center is vital to the continued growth of the Smithsonian and its collections.

The move of specimens and artifacts from the Museum of Natural History to the 4½-acre Center is a complex, multi-year project. Anthropological artifacts, entomology collections, botany specimens and countless "wet" collections—those stored in preserving fluids—have been cleaned, stabilized and transferred to one of the Support Center's four huge storage areas, known as "pods." Temperature and relative humidity in each pod is tightly controlled to provide optimum storage conditions.

Invaluable Conservation Research

Caring for the collections requires more than good storage conditions. Human skill and conservation research are essential. The 40-member staff of the Conservation Analytical Laboratory, located at the Support Center, conduct research on a wide variety of objects in the national collections, from ancient bronzes and ceramics to furniture, from spacesuits to paintings, textiles and paper artifacts.

The lab's activities are carried out in a number of interrelated programs: conservation treatment, conservation science, archaeometry, information and conservation training. Physical scientists, ar-

chaeologists and art historians in the Archaeometry Section focus on the origins, dates and production technology of objects and paintings.

In the Conservation Science Program, scientists, together with conservators in the Conservation Treatment Group, study the chemical and physical changes that occur as an object ages. A major goal is to find ways to stabilize materials and to prevent further deterioration. The conservators are also involved in the development of conservation treatment technology.

The Information Center staff is principally concerned with the assimilation of material published in the conservation field into a rapidly growing data base that is shared with conservators at other institutions. It also handles a large number of inquiries from the general public.

The Conservation Training Program offers internships and fellowships, as well as courses and

Harriet Beaubien, an objects conservator at the Conservation Analytical Laboratory, removes surface dirt from one of several lime plaster archaeological figures dating to the seventh millennium B.C., excavated at the site of 'Ain Ghazal, Jordan. (Photo by Doc Dougherty)

Tsang detail what happens when varnish and paint meet solvent, including such effects as swelling and leaching of the paint. They also measure changes in paint properties—hardness, color, gloss—caused by solvents and the effects of residual solvent on paint. Tsang provides an art historical perspective to this work, researching how paints and varnishes were applied in different periods of history, as well as the types of paint and materials used by different artists.

The project requires samples of many paint pigments, some of which are no longer commercially produced. Early in the project, then, specialists tracked down old paint recipes that include materials such as the lapis lazuli used in 12th-century paintings. Knowing how different paints change or degrade over time is also important. The susceptibility of paints to solvents may change as they age, Tsang says. By following changes in paint samples prepared for the project, the researchers can determine this and other potential problems that may arise when treating a painting.

Importance of Preservation

CAL staffers also carry out research in photograph preservation. Many old photographs and negatives have deteriorated over time, some to the point of destroying the captured image, photographic research scientist Mark McCormick-Goodhart says. This is true, for example, of the wet collodion process, an early method for making glass-plate negatives.

In this process, the photographer exposed and developed the image before the hand-poured light-sensitive coating was allowed to dry on the glass support. Surprisingly, recent results at CAL for collodion negatives made in Mathew Brady's Studios during the 1860s showed that seriously deteriorated images differed from those in fine condition due to the chemical composition of the glass on which they were coated. The photographers could not have foreseen the effect of 19th-century window glass on the life of their images!

"The materials and processes used in photography are so diverse that each type needs its own set of rules for conservation," McCormick-Goodhart says. Among the many collodion glass-plate negatives he works with are portraits of Abraham Lincoln by Alexander Gardner and Brady Studios images of such other prominent 19th-century figures as Ulysses S. Grant, Jefferson Davis, Samuel Morse and P. T. Barnum.

For accelerated-aging experiments, McCormick-Goodhart has re-created the collodion process in

workshops for practicing conservators. In addition, the Furniture Conservation Training Program is a four-year certificate course in furniture conservation that also offers a master's degree through Antioch University. Another effort, initiated jointly with Johns Hopkins University, offers graduate education in materials science at the master's and doctoral levels.

A recent example of the scope and importance of the laboratory's work focuses on the conservation of paintings, particularly on the solvents used to remove old deteriorated varnish applied as a protective coating. Solvents that remove varnish may also remove original paint in layers below the varnish. However, the definitive book on solvent action on varnishes is behind the times, having been published more than three decades ago.

To update this work and improve the conservation of paintings, CAL conservator Jia-Sun Tsang and a colleague, research chemist David Erhardt, have begun a project to evaluate "solvent systems" in order to eliminate or greatly reduce the potential for damaging a painting undergoing conservation. Using equipment such as CAL's gas chromatograph-mass spectrometer and its powerful scanning electron microscope, Erhardt and

THE SMITHSONIAN INSTITUTION: A WORLD OF DISCOVERY

his lab, learning to use the outdated technique to create new glass-plate negatives. Accelerated aging experiments on these plates, he says, will show how the negatives are affected by such environmental factors as temperature and humidity. This information will guide conservators and others in the care of historic collodion negatives in their collections. Re-creating the process will shed more light on the variations photographers applied to the basic technique.

Today's Technology Reveals the Past

Researchers at CAL also use today's technology to reveal detailed information about the past. One project involves the study of ancient Hopi pottery. Anthropologists Ron Bishop, Veletta Canouts and Suzanne De Atley examine the pottery, dating from the year 1300, for details about Hopi society and artistic traditions. The value of this effort is underlined by the fact that most of what is known about ancient Hopi history stems from oral legends. New information gained by the project is shared with today's Hopi, including students at Arizona's Hopi Junior-Senior High School who have worked on the project, as well as contemporary potters interested in lost Hopi techniques and traditions.

One technique the anthropologists hope to rediscover is the ancient Hopi method for achieving the distinctive yellow coloring of their pots. "Despite impurities in the clay," Canouts says, "the Hopi achieved the colors they wanted." An experimental kiln at CAL may eventually recover the lost technology.

Goals for the project also include learning more about ancient Hopi social organization, trading patterns and shared artistic traditions, as well as the impact of contact with the Spanish explorers in the 16th century. To that end, ceramic paste removed from the bottom of Hopi pots, many from the collections of the Museum of Natural History, is chemically analyzed with the aid of a nuclear reactor at the National Institute of Standards and Technology in Gaithersburg, Md.

Chemical profiles of the pots, Bishop explains, offer a wealth of data about pottery production and trading.

In addition to CAL, each Smithsonian art museum, as well as the Museum of American History, the Air and Space Museum and the Anthropology Department of the Museum of Natural History, has its own conservator or conservation department to serve the unique needs and problems of its collections.

Conserving a New Collection

In 1987, the new Sackler Gallery received its inaugural gift of nearly 1,000 objects of Asian and Near Eastern art. Each of these objects—most of them at least 1,000 years old—had to be examined and evaluated by curators and conservators before they were prepared for the opening exhibition.

Among the more memorable projects, according to head conservator Tom Chase, were 475 jades, heavily soiled from burial and centuries of handling; Syrian ivories from the first millennium B.C. that were literally turning to dust at every touch; and a 600-year-old Chinese tiered box made of once-shiny black lacquer that was flaking and intricate mother-of-pearl inlays that were loose, broken or missing. All of the pieces were rare and beautiful, but age and circumstances had punished them harshly.

In examining them as a necessary prelude to treatment, Chase and his colleagues used such methods as chemical analysis, thermoluminescence dating and X-ray diffraction to determine whether certain features of a piece were original or part of a previous restoration effort. Treatment, Chase says, must balance historical accuracy with aesthetics and common sense. For example, some green corrosion was left on a bronze vessel, providing an attractive contrast with the shiny bronze and a reminder of the object's great age.

Near Eastern silver pieces in the collection presented conservators with the greatest and most time-consuming challenges. Before beginning the work, the conservators took X-ray radiographs and examined the pieces under a microscope. Such care paid off. Consider the ancient rhyton, a ceremonial drinking vessel whose trumpet-shaped mouth piece had been crushed at some point in its history. To repair the damage, conservator Paul Jett annealed, or heated up, the metal and reshaped the rhyton around a wooden armature, using his hands so that he could feel any irregularities. Today, the rhyton seems unblemished.

Challenges of Conserving Modern Art

Modern art presents somewhat different challenges. General guidelines—for example, do not interfere with the artist's intent—still apply, Clarke Bedford, the Hirshhorn's conservator, says. "But for modern art, conservators may have very limited options."

Modern art, he explains, is often experimental. Artists use a wide mix of materials, including old hardware, newspapers, straw and adhesive, and they may mix acrylic and oil paints. As a result, "some works may tolerate very little treatment. You

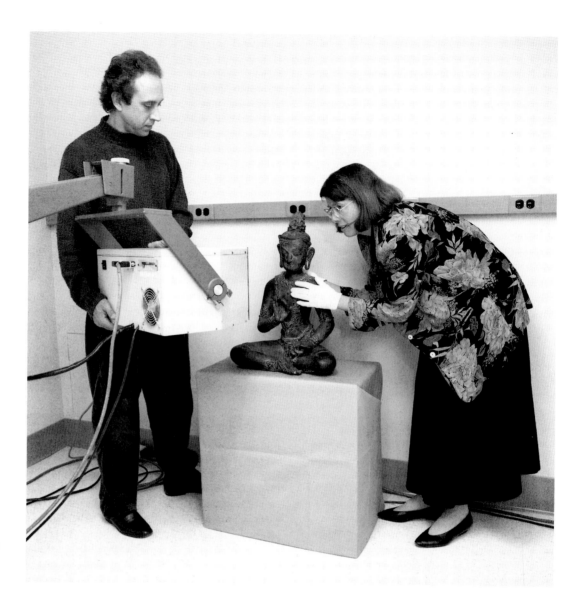

With new X-ray fluorescence equipment in the laboratory complex, conservators Paul Jett and Janet Douglas examine a Chinese lacquer sculpture displayed in the Freer Gallery, which reopened in 1993 after extensive renovation. (Photo by John Tsantes)

can't clean straw. Today's artists often are more interested in achieving an effect and not so interested in how long a work will last." In fact, Bedford adds, many artists may want their works to change or deteriorate over time. To restore such work to an original condition may be unacceptable.

Conserving Artifacts of Air and Space Technology

Icons of modern technology also require the unique skills of conservators and restoration experts. At the restoration shop of the Air and Space Museum's Paul E. Garber Facility—named for the late historian emeritus who helped acquire a large portion of the Smithsonian's aeronautical collection during his 70-year career—specialists work to restore artifacts of air and space history and to preserve the technology associated with these objects. The shop is located in one of 16 collection storage buildings at the facility, which holds the museum's reserve collection of more than 26,000 air and space artifacts, including such items from the Space Age as satellites, space probes and rockets.

Chances of preserving the technology of these objects have improved in recent years, shop foreman Richard Horigan says. With the advent of new techniques and new products and the refinement of old techniques, technicians can often save original paint, fabric, or mechanical and other parts of air- and spacecraft.

"Through dedication and lots of hard work, the shop preserves the technology associated with each artifact," Horigan says. Each project is unique. Some artifacts simply need to be cleaned up, while others require total restoration, down to the last nut and bolt. Replacing parts is a last resort, but when it is necessary, substitutes are fabricated and stamped as replicas. In a controlled museum environment, the restored object should last hundreds of years.

In addition to mastering outdated technology, members of the restoration team at the Garber Facility must familiarize themselves with the latest exotic alloys, metals and other materials, especially when restoring and preserving spacecraft, Horigan says. Projects under way or recently completed in the shop include restoration of a German World War II Arado 234, the world's first operational jet bomber; the Enola Gay, which changed the world when it dropped the first atom bomb on Hiroshima in 1945; a backup version of the Mariner 10 space probe; a structural dynamic model of the Hubble Space Telescope; and a Hawker Hurricane World War II British fighter.

Preserving and restoring the collections at the Garber Facility is the result of teamwork between the collections management staff and the museum's curators. The individual curator decides which objects should be restored or preserved and to what standards. "We try to ensure that the best possible treatments are given to the artifacts to ensure great-est longevity and to alter the object as little as possible," former senior curator Robert Mikesh says. "Weekly discussions between the curator, technician and conservator on the best methods to be followed are a must for this purpose."

He cites the work of two specialists on the HS-293 German guided missile used to strike Allied ships during World War II. They spent two months longer than anticipated restoring the warhead because of unforeseen corrosion and missing parts. It turned out to be far better constructed and more advanced technically than expected, requiring delicate handwork for restoration.

The largest project under way in the shop is the restoration of the B-29 Enola Gay, carrier of the first atom bomb. In the July 1988 issue of Smithsonian magazine, Robert McC. Adams, secretary of the Smithsonian Institution, pointed to the importance of restoring this plane for eventual public display. "The significance of most human artifacts found in museums lies safely in the past.... However, certain objects erase the possibility of detachment. Icons of the atomic age are one of these."

Conservators at the Air and Space Museum's Garber Facility exercise exceptional skills and historic sleuthing to restore aircraft.

THE JOURNEY CONTINUES: DIFFUSING THE FRUITS OF RESEARCH

Selected Smithsonian Programs

That Contribute

to the Diffusion of Knowledge

Each year, the Smithsonian produces videotapes and recordings that help diffuse the fruits of its research projects. (Photo by Eric Long)

Among the most visible results of Smithsonian research are the hundreds of books, magazines and brochures that are produced each year. (Photo by Eric Long)

The Smithsonian's first benefactor, James Smithson, believed that the advancement of knowledge would provide opportunities for the social and moral improvement of humankind. But he also understood that it was not enough merely to increase knowledge. Rather, as an equal partner in the Smithsonian's two-part mission, diffusion of that knowledge from the Smithsonian's myriad research efforts must also reach the broadest possible audience.

In the early days of the Institution, and for many years after, the Smithsonian was virtually the sole active research organization in the United States. Joseph Henry, the Smithsonian's first secretary, felt a special obligation to communicate with other like-minded organizations around the world. The first in a series of *Smithsonian Contributions to Knowledge,* an investigation of American Indian mounds published only two years after the Smithsonian was established, launched an uninterrupted flow of original research reports still in demand around the globe. Smithsonian scholars continue to publish thousands of pages of their research in the most prestigious scholarly publications and Smithsonian monographs. Smithsonian researchers also present their research to their counterparts around the world annually in hundreds of public and scholarly lectures, seminars and symposia, thereby fostering international cooperation and sharing in basic research and museum programs.

Today, however, the Smithsonian diffuses its research around the world in ways that could not have been dreamed of by James Smithson. A vast network of behind-the-scenes staff members from several dozen offices underpin Smithsonian research and its dissemination, from the Smithsonian Institution Libraries, Smithsonian Institution Archives and various other archives to its visitor and media information services providing information to the public and journalists to promote understanding of the newest research findings.

Because its mission is the increase and diffusion of knowledge, the Smithsonian is particularly positioned to connect the scholarly world of inquiry, experiment, creativity and invention with the many-faceted world of the public.

Public Outreach

Several hundred exhibitions—perhaps the most public manifestation of Smithsonian research—open in the Smithsonian's museums each year. In addition, the Smithsonian Institution Traveling Exhibition Service and the museums themselves extend the results of Smithsonian research beyond the walls of their own museums to cities and towns across the United States and around the world. At any one time, more than 100 exhibitions in art, history, science and technology are traveling to museums, galleries, colleges, cultural institutions, and other public centers at home and abroad.

The Smithsonian Institution Press, like exhibitions, is a direct link between research scholarship and the public. The University Press Division publishes texts for scholars, while the Smithsonian Books Division publishes popular and fascinating works richly illustrated with color photographs that interpret the mysteries of scholarship in language understandable to the lay public. This division publishes dozens of titles each year.

The Smithsonian Institution Press also publishes sound and video recordings using the latest electronic technologies to enhance the traditional dissemination of knowledge through printed books. It is joined in these efforts by such offices as the Office of Telecommunications which extends the reach of the Smithsonian through nationally broadcast television and radio programs, educational films and home video.

Worth 10,000 Words

Photographic imagery in all forms, from stills to digital discs, has become the common currency both of research and the dissemination of knowledge. The Office of Printing and Photographic Services is the Smithsonian's image bank, a treasury of hundreds of thousands of master images, that documents the growing national collections and the Smithsonian's research and other activities. Many images are, or soon will be, available on laser disks and via computer to members of the media, as well as the public, through downloading on their personal computers.

The Smithsonian Institution is an unusual "open university," with innovative educational opportunities throughout the nation. Through The Smithsonian Associates, the Smithsonian offers the local Washington, D.C., community a rich mix of continuing education programs, including courses, studio arts, lectures, seminars, films, performing arts and study tours. Nationally, more than 2 million Smithsonian Associates can take advantage of a similar menu in cities around the world. Smithsonian Research Expeditions give members the chance to help increase knowledge by working directly with Smithsonian scholars on research projects, and Smithsonian Study Tours allow Associates opportunities to visit places throughout the world, guided by Smithsonian scholars.

Smithsonian Associates also receive as a benefit of membership Smithsonian magazine, a monthly treasure chest of articles that reflect the full breadth of Smithsonian interests and the diversity of the nation. Its sister publication, Air & Space/Smithsonian magazine keeps its readers up to date on the latest happenings of the Air and Space Age.

The Smithsonian takes its obligations seriously to share its research resources with future generations. It does so directly, through its extensive graduate and postgraduate fellowship and undergraduate and high-school internship programs, and through its symposia, seminars, workshops, school programs and curriculum materials designed for teachers, students and museum professionals. While every museum, every research facility and nearly every corner of the Smithsonian takes part in these activities through individual programs, coordination and support are provided by the offices of Museum Programs, Fellowships and Grants, Elementary and Secondary Education, and International Relations. The National Science Resources Center holds school Leadership Institutes and serves as a clearinghouse and developer for precollege science curriculum materials, and the Smithsonian Astrophysical Observatory has a cooperative program with Harvard University that has developed astronomy-based high-school curriculum materials.

In 1996, the Smithsonian will celebrate its 150th anniversary. The Smithsonian's founder believed that the challenges for the increase and diffusion of knowledge lay everywhere. Then, as now, Smithsonian scholars are on a never-ending quest for new knowledge and understanding. They toil in the conservation laboratories of art museums; they travel to the abyssal depths of the ocean; they contemplate worlds at unimaginably distant edges of the universe—all the time following a tradition of expanding frontiers of knowledge. As Joseph Henry, the Smithsonian's first secretary, said, "The way of discovery gives us a higher point of view for making excursions into the regions of the unknown," a world of discovery that continues to grow and enlarge for the benefit of all people.

SMITHSONIAN INSTITUTION

SECRETARY
Office of Inspector General

UNDER SECRETARY
Office of the General Counsel
Office of Government Relations
Office of Public Affairs
Office of Policy and Program Development

ARTS AND HUMANITIES
Office of the Assistant Secretary for the Arts and Humanities
Anacostia Museum
Archives of American Art
Arthur M. Sackler Gallery
Cooper-Hewitt, National Museum of Design
Freer Gallery of Art
Hirshhorn Museum and Sculpture Garden
Institutional Studies Office
National Air and Space Museum
National Museum of African Art
National Museum of American Art
   Renwick Gallery
National Museum of American History
   National Postal Museum
National Museum of the American Indian
National Portrait Gallery
Office of Exhibits Central
Office of Museum Programs
Smithsonian Institution Traveling Exhibition Service

EDUCATION AND PUBLIC SERVICE
Office of the Assistant Secretary for Education and Public Service
Center for Folklife Programs and Cultural Studies
National Science Resources Center
Office of Elementary and Secondary Education

EXTERNAL AFFAIRS
Office of the Assistant Secretary for External Affairs
Office of International Relations
Office of Special Events and Conference Services
Office of Telecommunications
Smithsonian Institution Press
Smithsonian Magazine
Air & Space/Smithsonian Magazine
The Smithsonian Associates
Visitor Information and Associates' Reception Center

FINANCE AND ADMINISTRATION
Office of the Assistant Secretary for Finance and Administration
Business Management Office
   Concessions
   Mail Order Division
   Office of Product Development and Licensing
   Smithsonian Museum Shops
Office of the Comptroller
Office of Contracting and Property Management
Office of Equal Employment
   and Minority Affairs
Office of Facilities Services
   Office of Architectural History
      and Historic Preservation
   Office of Design and Construction
   Office of Environmental Management and Safety
   Office of Plant Services
   Office of Protection Services
Office of Financial and Management Analysis
Office of Human Resources
Office of Information Resource Management
Office of Planning and Budget
Office of Printing and Photographic Services
Office of Risk Management
Office of Sponsored Projects
Office of the Treasurer
Travel Services Office

INSTITUTIONAL INITIATIVES
Office of the Assistant Secretary for Institutional Initiatives
National Campaign for the National Museum
   of the American Indian
Office of Development

SCIENCES
Office of the Assistant Secretary for the Sciences
Conservation Analytical Laboratory
National Museum of Natural History
   Museum Support Center
National Zoological Park
Office of Fellowships and Grants
Smithsonian Astrophysical Observatory
Smithsonian Environmental Research Center
Smithsonian Institution Archives
Smithsonian Institution Libraries
Smithsonian Tropical Research Institute